Challenges from a New World

George Walker

Published in 2010 by John Catt Educational Ltd
Unit 12, Deben Mill Business Centre, Melton, Woodbridge, Suffolk IP12 1BL, UK
Tel: +44 (0) 1394 389850 Fax: +44 (0) 1394 386893
Email: enquiries@johncatt.com Website: www.johncatt.com

Managing Director: Jonathan Evans. Editor-in-Chief: Derek Bingham

Challenges from a New World © John Catt Educational Ltd 2010
All rights reserved.

No part of this publication may be reproduced, stored in a retrieval system, transmitted in any form or by any means, electronic, mechanical, photocopying, recording, or otherwise, without the prior permission of the publishers.

Opinions expressed in this publication are those of the contributors and are not necessarily those of the publishers or the sponsors. We cannot accept responsibility for any errors or omissions.

The Sex Discrimination Act of 1975.

The publishers have taken all reasonable steps to avoid a contravention of Section 38 of the Sex Discrimination Act 1975. However, it should be noted that (save where there is an express provision to the contrary) where words have been used which denote the masculine gender only, they shall, pursuant and subject to the said Act, for the purpose of this publication, be deemed to include the feminine gender and *vice versa*.

ISBN: 978 1 904724 79 7

Set and designed by
John Catt Educational Ltd

Printed and bound in Great Britain by
Bell & Bain Ltd, Glasgow, Scotland

Contents

Introduction   5

International Education: Response to a Previous World   7
Reprinted by permission of Sage Publications Ltd, from
The SAGE Handbook of Research in International Education, *Mary Hayden, Jack Levey, Jeff Thompson (eds), London 2007*

Educating the Global Citizen   20
Renaissance College, Hong Kong, 16 August 2007

Review of *Five Minds for the Future*   33
by Howard Gardner
Boston MA: Harvard Business School Press, 2006
First published in the Journal for Research in International Education, *December 2007, volume 6.3, and reprinted here with permission from Sage Publications Ltd.*

Education: for the Nation or for the World?   38
Chautauqua Institution, New York, 4 July 2006

Schools as Cultural Crossroads   51
International School of Geneva, 7 January 2006

Global Warming   63
25th Opening Ceremony of United World College of the Adriatic
Teatro Verdi, Trieste, 20 October 2007

The Sky's the Limit   69
International Baccalaureate Academic Staff Seminar, Cardiff
31 March 2008

Teaching for Quality Education: the Example of Mr Chips   75
Conference of British Schools in the Middle East, Muscat
31 January 2007

Doing No Harm   83
TASIS, Lugano, 26 March 2009

Think Globally; Act Locally   93
Graduation of the Campus des Nations, International School of Geneva
12 June 2009

Contents

Introduction 5

International Education Responses to a Fractious World 7
Reprinted by permission of Sage Publications Ltd. from
the SAGE Handbook of Research in International Education, Mary
Hayden, Jack Levy, Jeff Thompson (eds), London 2007

Educating the Global Citizen 20
Beadle-one-r College, Hong Kong, 16 January 2007

Review of Five Minds for the Future 33
by Howard Gardner
(Boston, MA: Harvard Business School Press, 2006)
First published in the Journal of Research in International Education
December 2007 Volume 6 Number 3 and reprinted here with permission from
Sage Publications Ltd.

Education: the Nation or for the World? 38
Centenary Lectures, Beijing, 4-6 May 2006

Schools as Cultural Crossroads 51
International School of Trieste, 2 August 2006

Global Stewardship ....
XXIV Commencement Address of United World College of the Adriatic,
Trieste, 26 October 200

The Sky's the Limit 69
International Baccalaureate Americas Ann Seminar, Canada,
5-7 March 2006

Leadership for Family Education: the Example of Mao Zetong 75
Xiangtan and Hunan Normal University, Hunan, East Meeting
14 January 2006

Being Be-Dared 83
ONSC London, 26 March 2007

Think Globally, Act Locally 93
Conference of the Canadian Confederation, International School of Geneva,
12 June 2006

Introduction

Challenges from a New World

International education grew up during the 20th century, partly to support the increasing global mobility of professional families and partly as a response to the appalling bloodshed and destruction of two world wars. By the end of the century it had come of age, no longer needing explanation or justification as it began to spread its influence into the mainstream public systems of education.

Perhaps 'getting to know you' best sums up the achievements of its first period of development. A deeper understanding of the lifestyles, the languages and the aspirations of people living in distant lands would lead to more effective trade, to more productive diplomacy and, some argued, to a more peaceful world. International education has always displayed both pragmatic and visionary dimensions.

When I retired from the International Baccalaureate (IB) in 2006 it was clear that the 21st century was presenting new challenges. For example, modern transportation and communication had rendered largely meaningless the phrase 'living in distant lands' and whatever conflict lay ahead it was rather unlikely to fit the term 'world war'. 'Effective trade' now seemed to have only a tenuous relationship with 'productive diplomacy' as new and sometimes unmanageable forces started to drive the world's economies, rather like the jet stream drives our weather.

Perhaps the appropriate motto for early 21st century international education will be 'getting to live with you' as the growing diversity caused by mass immigration challenges the cultural cohesion of many nation states. Some are divided internally by ethnic conflicts, which have violent knock-on effects far from the country of origin.

Indeed, the very concept of a nation state (and without a nation what is our understanding of the term 'international'?) is being slowly eroded by the phenomenon that we call 'globalization'. A nation's capacity to act independently in the realms of politics, economics and social affairs has been greatly compromised as countries across the globe become linked together in a partially completed and often poorly fitting jigsaw puzzle of inter-related demography, economy and culture.

In apparent contrast, it seems that education has remained one of the few levers still under the control of individual national governments, which are still very sensitive to comparative international league tables of educational achievement. But what kind of education, what knowledge, skills and values, do young people need in the 21st century to live active, fulfilled lives in this New World?

Surprisingly little has been written about the impact of globalization on education, perhaps because it is still too early to see with any clarity just what the effect might be. Since my retirement from the IB I have seized every opportunity in speeches, articles and book reviews to examine some of the issues that will face international educators in the 21st century, including:

- students' understanding of the concept of globalization;
- the multicultural nature of most contemporary societies;
- rapid, unmediated access to complex information;
- unethical behaviour that puts free-market democracies at risk;
- the threat to the planet of global warming; and
- the growing world influence of non-western countries with different cultural priorities.

None of these would have found a place in a list of top ten concerns much before the final decade of the 20th century. Now, they have become the most demanding issues that education *must* address at the start of the 21st century.

George Walker

International Education: Response to a Previous World

International education put down its first enduring roots in 1924, with the opening of the International School of Geneva (École Internationale de Genève). Ecolint, as it became known, fulfilled the practical need of providing an education for the multinational children of the new breed of international civil servants working at the League of Nations. But its founders had more complex ambitions, namely to instil into these young people the same values of international understanding and tolerance that were enshrined in the League's own Covenant. In this way, perhaps, there would be no repetition of the carnage of the First World War. International education could help the process of nation speaking to nation.

The school's style of education was far ahead of its time and a radical suggestion, made by the chairman of its governing board in 1925, proposing an international school leaving certificate, fell on deaf ears. But the most telling blow to its visionary ambitions came with the outbreak of the Second World War. Nonetheless, it survived and, when the war was over, Ecolint helped to found a sister school with similar aspirations in New York, the United Nations International School (UNIS). This postwar period saw a rapid growth of international schools, matching the expansion of world trade, the associated support of diplomatic missions and the steady growth of international agencies, many of them linked to the United Nations. Some of these so-called 'international schools' maintained an unashamedly national (particularly American and British) education set down in the midst of foreign, sometimes even hostile, countries far from home. But others were inspired by the example of Ecolint and UNIS to develop something new, something more visionary, something that would perhaps ensure the world would never again see horrors such as those of the Second World War. International education could help to foster a new spirit of international tolerance.

These mushrooming international schools were soon given practical support in their mission by their own organization, the International Schools Association (ISA), established in 1951 in close association with the recently founded United Nations Educational, Scientific and Cultural Organization (UNESCO), by parents who were international civil servants working in Geneva, New York and Paris. Predictably, the ISA reinforced the visionary aspect of international education and the first aim in its current mission statement remains 'To further world peace and international understanding through education'.[1]

Ten years later another event had a profound effect on the developing international school movement: the opening, in 1962, of Atlantic College in Wales. By now memories of the Second World War were fading, but only to be replaced by the superpower tensions of the Cold War, with its ever-present threat of wholesale nuclear destruction. Surely, it was argued, a residential experience, founded on the experiential philosophy of Kurt Hahn – 'an enterprising curiosity, an undefeatable spirit, tenacity in pursuit, readiness for sensible self denial, and above all, compassion'[2] – an experience that offered the world's brightest and best teenagers the opportunity to live and study for two years, amongst a complete mix of different cultures and backgrounds and to make lifelong friendships across sometimes forbidden national frontiers, surely this would somehow reduce the chances of another world war. Thus, with the creation of the first United World College, the visionary dimension of international education that had been promoted 40 years earlier in Geneva was further reinforced. Schools, and the young people in them, could transcend the barriers of even the Cold War's frontiers.

International education in a changing social environment

To be a realistic alternative to national, or state, education, international education must coexist with existing social, economic and political structures. It must fulfil a practical need; institutions offering it must become established and attract suitable staff; governments must at least accept, if not welcome it, and its curriculum and qualifications must be widely recognized. All these conditions were satisfied during the rapid development of international education taking place in the last century. Moreover, international education went further, seeming to offer at least a response, if not a solution, to some of the most pressing moral challenges of a century ravaged by war.

However, at the beginning of the 21st century, the social environment of education is changing in response to the accelerating processes of globalization and to the ever widening participation of new educational stakeholders. Hitherto, international education has been largely concerned with the relationships between groups contained within different geographical boundaries; indeed, as we have seen, its origins lay in the initiatives taken by international schools to encourage mutual understanding between different nation-states. However, as immigration once more shifting the position of education along the internal-external axis as groups (for example the business community) that have stronger international sympathies and experience, assume a degree of responsibility for the provision of education.

Internal education is merging with external education and all this is taking place against the trends of increasing migration and ease of communication. This, in turn, implies that an education to understand different cultures living in other countries will, in future, have to be modified to take into account different cultures living just down the road, often using new technology in ways that make it unimportant where they are living.

The new global challenges

International education aimed to bring about the meeting of nations: rubbing shoulders, building tolerance and lifting the barriers of national frontiers. All this has a 20th century ring to it, but it is less relevant in the 21st century where nations already rub shoulders daily in a thousand different ways, international forums (albeit far from perfect) exist to resolve disputes causing international tension and very few countries remain off limits to the committed traveller. The challenge of the new century is not to bring people of different cultures together, but to address some of the issues that arise when this happens on a daily, hourly, minute-by-minute basis, thanks to the impact of globalization.

What are the particular global challenges for the century that lies ahead and how can international education help to meet them? Suárez-Orozco suggests that working with difference and complexity will be particularly important keys to understanding the future. On the former, he emphasizes not just meeting together, but living together, often in the closest proximity:

> Children growing up today are more likely than in any previous generation to face a life of working, networking, loving, and living with others from different national, linguistic, religious and racial backgrounds... The friction that meaningful cultural contact and incommensurable difference generate can be a threat if mismanaged – as intergroup violence and anomie in multicultural cities suggest. But friction can also generate constructive energy ... When intercultural difference interrupts 'thinking as usual' – the taken for granted understandings and world views that shape cognitive and metacognitive styles and practices – it can do most for youths growing up today.[3]

On complexity, Suárez-Orozco writes:

> Globalization engenders complexity. It is generating more intricate demographies, economies, politics, environmental choices, scientific realities, technology and media, cultural facts and artefacts, and identities... An intellectually curious, cognitively autonomous, socially responsible, democratically engaged, productive, and globally conscious member of the human family in the 21st century cannot be educated in the 20th-century factory model of education.[4]

Gardner expresses similar sentiments and reflects on the implications for the school curriculum:

> Many – perhaps most – of the most vexing issues facing the world today (including the issue of globalization!) do not respect disciplinary boundaries. AIDS, large-scale immigration, and global warming are examples of problems in need of interdisciplinary thinking. How best to begin to introduce rigorous multi-perspective thinking into our classrooms is a challenge that we have only begun to confront.[5]

And his first priority for the future is an understanding of the new realities of the global system itself:

> The trends of globalization – the unprecedented and unpredictable movement of human beings, capital, information, and cultural life forms – need to be understood by the young persons who are and will always inhabit a global community. Some of the system will become manifest through the media; but many other facets – for example, the operation of worldwide markets – will need to be taught in a more formal manner.[6]

Friedman[7] makes a similar point in his analysis of the forces that have 'flattened' the worlds of business, commerce and education. His conclusions make equally uncomfortable reading for the Old World and the New World as he predicts the steady erosion of their current competitive advantages as countries like India, China and Russia seize the new opportunities offered by what he calls a triple convergence: the power of the internet, changes in practices that reflect new and more efficient ways of doing business and the consequent addition of some three billion new people to competitive markets. For Friedman, the reconciliation of widening capitalism with the fate of its seemingly inevitable victims, lies in a form of 'compassionate flatism' in which education will play an essential part.

Friedman's argument that the balance of global power is shifting away from the West (as he points out, to be 'one in a million' in China is to be part of a group numbering 1300) is derived from an essentially economic perspective: 'The jobs are going to go where the best educated workforce is with the most competitive infrastructure and environment for creativity and supportive government. It is inevitable.'[8]

Jacques agrees:

> We are moving into a world in which the West will no longer be able to call the tune as it once did. China and India will becomes major global players alongside the US, the EU and Japan. For the first time in modern history the West will no longer be overwhelmingly dominant.[9]

But he adds a moral dimension to the argument:

> It is no longer possible for Europe to ignore the sensibilities of peoples with very different values, cultures and religions. First, Western Europe now has sizeable minorities whose origins are very different from the host population and who are connected with their former homelands in diverse ways. If European societies want to live in some kind of domestic peace and harmony ... then they must find ways of integrating these minorities on rather more equal terms than, for the most part, they have so far achieved.[10]

The shock generated by the London bombings in July 2005 and the destructive rioting in the suburbs of many French cities that occurred later in the year, was due not only to their happening but also to the uncomfortable fact that they were caused by national citizens rather than malevolent outsiders.

Rischard[11] lists no fewer than 20 global issues that, in his opinion, must be resolved in the next 20 years. They are grouped into three categories: those that have to do with sharing the global living space (*eg* global warming), social and economic issues (*eg* world poverty), whose solution requires 'a critical mass that only global coalitions can achieve', and legal and regulatory issues (*eg* intellectual property rights) that demand a common rule book. Rischard argues that the world lacks effective mechanisms for dealing with these issues and, indeed, his main thesis is that current institutions have not kept pace with either world demographic or world economic changes.

In summary, then, these are what experts perceive to be the new challenges of the 21st century:

- Living and working with difference – kinship, gender, language, race, ethnicity and inequality; therefore interrupting the process of 'thinking as usual'.
- Enjoying the challenge of complexity, which means assessing problems from a variety of different perspectives and accepting the absence of a single solution.
- Acquiring a better understanding of the driving forces behind globalization and its impact on different groups; understanding, for example, the interconnectivity of buying habits.
- Recognizing that the balance of economic power in the world is shifting to different parts of the world and that, increasingly, education will be the determinant of economic success.
- Coping with cultural differences, not as a visitor or expatriate in another country, but on a daily, and sometimes potentially confrontational, basis at one's own back door.
- Seeking new styles of working that do not depend upon outdated and inefficient institutions that were designed for a previous era.

To what extent, then, does international education, as currently practised, prepare young people for these new challenges?

International education in practice: the International Baccalaureate

The curriculum and the associated values of international education were formalized, institutionalized and made available worldwide with the creation of the International Baccalaureate Organization (IBO) in 1968. This initiative, which was supervised by the ISA and funded by UNESCO and a number of American foundations, was largely driven by teachers in schools like Ecolint, UNIS and Atlantic College, working together to solve that frustrating problem anticipated some 40 years earlier – the creation of an international pre-university programme that could be studied anywhere in the world and providing access to any of the world's best universities. The result was the IB Diploma Programme, a values-inspired response to a practical problem.[12]

Nearly two generations later, that programme has achieved its early, ambitious goal to a remarkable degree yet still retains much of the overall shape with which it was launched.[13] Three influences largely determined its design: the idealism represented by ISA and UNESCO, the classroom experience of subject specialist teachers and the requirements of university admissions tutors. The result was a compromise: an intellectually demanding liberal arts programme with a strong international dimension, an emphasis on critical thinking skills, the encouragement of foreign languages and an insistence on community service. Several of its constituent parts, notably the Theory of Knowledge course, the compulsory element of Creativity, Action, Service (CAS) and the extended essay, continue to attract widespread interest, but it is the diploma's overall shape, carefully designed to be more than just the sum of those constituent parts, that remains so distinctive, even today.

For more than a generation, its Diploma Programme maintained the IBO in a small but increasingly influential niche position, winning recognition by offering a welcomed passport to the world's most sought-after universities. Surprisingly, and for some international purists, somewhat annoyingly, the greatest rate of growth was in the USA, where public schools, not especially interested in its international nature, were attracted to a high-quality programme with internationally benchmarked assessment. But the capacity to infiltrate state systems has been crucial to its development and many different governments have taken an interest in the IB Diploma Programme, incorporating elements of it within their own national programmes.[14]

During the 1990s, in the most significant developments since its founding, the IBO added a Middle Years Programme and then a Primary Years Programme, thereby greatly widening the organization's role and responsibilities. From that moment the IBO has made the running in the development of international education: indeed, it has been suggested[15] that the IB programmes might even be regarded as the educational global equivalent of Nike or Coca-Cola. In practice, for many schools across the world, participation in international education has meant authorization to offer one or more of the IB programmes – for them international education has become synonymous with the IB. It is therefore not unreasonable to rephrase the earlier question, so as to ask how relevant the IB programmes will be in preparing young people for the globalized world of the 21st century.

According to Suárez-Orozco and Qin-Hilliard: 'Education systems tied to the formation of nation-state citizens and consumers bonded to local systems to the neglect of larger global forces are likely to become obsolete, while those that proactively engage globalization's new challenges are likely to survive.'[16] Clearly, the IBO was itself a direct response to a global force – increasing international trade – and the programmes' different international dimensions, including the study of modern languages and world literature as well as its international teams of curriculum developers and examiners, mean that it is not bonded to any local system. However, to what extent do the programmes: 'proactively engage globalization's new challenges?'

Gardner specifically commends the Theory of Knowledge course as an appropriate basis for an introduction to interdisciplinary work, and the so-called 'areas of interaction', which form an important interdisciplinary focus in the IB Middle Years Programme, offer a similar opportunity to examine a particular issue from a variety of disciplinary standpoints. Developing cultural understanding also plays an essential part in all three IB programmes but this is usually in an international context where engagement is often temporary and optional, rather than the local context of an immigrant group that constitutes a growing minority on the other side of the same city. IB students in the Midlands or North of England are more likely to choose French, Spanish or *ab initio* Japanese as their foreign language than Urdu or Gujarati.

One of the strengths of the 20th century model of the IB has been its close association with schools. Teachers and administrators have contributed to every aspect and at every level of the organization: developing the curriculum, training new teachers, lobbying governments, examining students and participating in its governance. In the future, however, this strength could become a serious weakness if IB programmes remain exclusively bound to particular institutions. The successful spread of educational opportunity to match the new distribution of economic wealth does not imply the death of schools, but it does mean that they will become just one part of a much wider and varied network of education providers, all making use of the latest technology.

Acquiring responsibility for three programmes of international education – kindergarten to grade 12 – has encouraged the IBO to engage in an extensive study of the key factors that underpin them, in a search for a more generic description of what the IB represents: what are the common threads that are progressively developed from elementary schooling through to pre-university graduation, the essential ingredients of this version of an international education? They have been expressed in the so-called 'IB learner profile',[17] which, perhaps unsurprisingly, restates many of the qualities that were in the minds of the early pioneers: for example, critical thinking, communication, caring and reflecting. The list of ten chosen qualities divides roughly into two categories, which could be said to reflect the nature of the IB experience itself and thus of much of the current practice of international education: a critical mind linked to a compassionate heart.

Perhaps this is the description of the social entrepreneur; indeed Friedman himself writes:

> I have come to know several social entrepreneurs in recent years and most combine a business school brain with a social worker's heart.[18]

Bornstein,[19] noting that during the 1990s the number of registered international citizen organizations (not-for-profit organizations with a global influence) increased from 6000 to 26,000, suggests that several factors are encouraging the worldwide mobilization of citizens: the replacement of many authoritarian governments, surplus wealth in many economies (albeit very unevenly distributed), greater longevity and better education, more extensive participation of women and new forms of technology.

It seems likely that the IB graduates will have a particular contribution to make to what could become a really significant movement of the new century:

> Across the world, social entrepreneurs are demonstrating new approaches to many social ills and new models to create wealth, promote social wellbeing, and restore the environment. The citizen sector is conspicuously leading the push to reform the free market and political systems.[20]

Because unarguably there is deep disillusion concerning the capacity of governments to address and solve the growing list of serious global problems, and private enterprise is widely perceived as making a bad situation worse.

However, a final word of caution is needed because 'business school brains' and 'social worker hearts' are both very western phrases. They describe concepts that fit comfortably with the IB and its model of international education, which is founded upon a western humanist philosophy that encourages freedom of speech, challenges authority and rewards individual initiative:

> The configuration of learning presumed in international academic curricula is a Western configuration based on conceptual learning as the dominant form of learning.[21]

Those from different cultural backgrounds may reason differently and attach different priorities to what they value in their society. Unable to match business school brains to social worker hearts, and fearing social and economic marginalization as the global economy further reinforces the power of western capitalism, their difference is being expressed with increasing emphasis, sometimes with increasing violence, around the world.

The final sentence of the IBO's mission statement insists that:

> These [IB] programmes encourage students across the world to become active, compassionate and lifelong learners who understand that other people, with their differences, can also be right.[22]

Just how right 'other people, with their differences' will be allowed to be, and just how right these other people will insist on being, are issues that will surely pose the biggest future challenge to international education. If international education is really preparing young people to face the new rather than the past century, then it will start by recognizing that in the West:

> [T]oo many young people have a sense of entitlement, are complacent and even condescending towards the rest of the world and this could be our downfall.[23]

References

1. International Schools Association (2006): www.isaschools.org (accessed 20 July 2006).
2. Hahn, K. (2006): www.KurtHahn.org (accessed 20 March 2006).
3. Suárez-Orozco, M. M. (2005): Rethinking education in the global era, in *Phi Delta Kappan*, 87(3): 209–12.
4. *ibid.*
5. Gardner, H. (2004): How education changes: considerations of history, science and values, in M. M. Suárez-Orozco and D. B. Qin-Hilliard (eds): *Globalization: Culture and Education in the New Millennium*. Berkeley, CA: University of California Press.
6. *ibid.*
7. Friedman, T. (2005): *The World Is Flat*. London: Allen Lane.
8. *ibid.*
9. Jacques, M. (2006): Europe's contempt for other cultures can't be sustained, in the *Guardian*, 17 February 2006.
10. *ibid.*
11. Rischard, J. F. (2002): *High Noon*. New York: Basic Books.
12. Peterson, A. D. C. (1987): *Schools Across Frontiers*. La Salle: Open Court.

13. International Baccalaureate Organization (IBO) (2006): www.ibo.org (accessed 18 March 2006).
14. Hill, I. (2007): International Baccalaureate programmes and educational reform, in P. Hughes (ed.): *Secondary Education at the Crossroads*. Dordrecht: Springer (in press).
15. Cambridge, J. (2002): Global product branding and international education, in the *Journal of Research in International Education*, 1(2): 227–43.
16. Suárez-Orozco, M. M. and Qin-Hilliard, D. B. (eds) (2004): *Globalization: Culture and Education in the New Millennium*. Berkeley, CA: University of California Press.
17. IBO (2006): www.ibo.org (accessed 18 March 2006).
18. Friedmand, T. (2005): *The World is Flat*. London: Allen Lane.
19. Bornstein, D. (2004): *How to Change the World*. Oxford: Oxford University Press.
20. *ibid.*
21. Van Oord, L. (2005): Culture as a configuration of learning: hypotheses in the context of international education, in the *Journal of Research in International Education*, 4(2): 173–91
22. IBO (2006): www.ibo.org (accessed 18 March 2006).
23. Seefried, M. (2005): Speech to South Carolina IB Association. www.ibo.org (accessed 20 July 2006).

Educating the Global Citizen

Renaissance College, Hong Kong
16 August 2007

Belonging

One of the most powerful human instincts is the need to belong. Our membership of families, of organizations and of societies shapes our identity. It defines who we are and, to a large extent, it determines who we shall become.

Anyone picking up my wallet in the street would find immediate evidence of my belonging: two different banks, the Royal Society for the Arts, the local library, the University of Bath, the National Trust and the East India Club in London – all linked to different parts of my life. My diary would give further clues, particularly of my family. My passport confirms my nationality and my membership of the European Union.

In the end, all these different belongings – they have been called 'threads of affiliation' – weave together, mostly harmoniously but sometimes with friction, to make up our culture. And our culture has been called the 'software of our mind', reminding us how powerfully we have become culturally programmed to respond in particular ways to particular situations.

One of our most public belongings is to a nation; it is stamped on our passport, the document that confirms our official identity. But nationality has never been a fixed, stable characteristic and the whole concept of a nation is historically quite new. I need not remind an audience in Hong Kong that you can go to bed belonging to one nation and wake up in the morning as a member of another. An exact match of land, language and culture was rare enough in the past but today mass migration and the creation of economic and political super-states like the European Union call further into question the relevance of the word 'nation'.

And yet the United Nations continues to expand, adding 35 nations in the last 25 years, including seven in the last ten years, and our definition of an economically viable nation has changed to include many of surprisingly small size. In practice, though, a nation will contain groups of diverse ethnic origins, each determined to preserve, indeed to strengthen, its cultural identity as manifested by language, customs and tradition. In my own country, for example, the union flag and the national anthem are slowly beginning to appear outdated as political devolution encourages people to belong to Scotland, Wales and Northern Ireland rather than the United Kingdom.

The supremacy of the nation may be weakening, eroded by supra-national blocs on the one hand and diverse ethnic groupings on the other, but it retains one trump card: citizenship. It is to the nation that citizens owe their allegiance and it is from the nation that citizens claim their protection. And it is through education that nations try to shape their future citizens, giving them selected knowledge and skills, inculcating selected ethical values and transmitting selected elements of the national culture.

World citizenship

Not surprisingly then, education has always been regarded as an inescapable national responsibility and despite many debates in the 1920s, the League of Nations in Geneva refused to have anything to do with it, arguing that there could be no international approach to education. It was not until 1946 that the United Nations became involved through the creation of UNESCO, whose founding fathers may have remembered a powerful speech by US President Roosevelt a year earlier, when he said:

> And so today, in this year of war ... we have learned lessons – at a fearful cost – and we shall profit by them.
>
> We have learned that we cannot live alone, at peace; that our own well-being is dependent on the well-being of other nations far away. We have learned that we must live as men, not as ostriches, nor as dogs in the manger.
>
> We have learned to be citizens of the world, members of the human community.'

In that brief passage from his fourth inaugural speech, Roosevelt describes a new kind of citizen, the citizen of the world, with the double explanation:

- we all belong to the same human community
- we cannot expect to live alone in peace,

which captures the two essential elements of world citizenship, one philosophical and the other political.

Let us take a brief look at the philosophical dimension because the idea of belonging to a single human community is not new. In the 4th century BC, Diogenes the Cynic, when asked where he came from, replied, 'I am a citizen of the world', using for the first time the word 'cosmopolitan'. The Roman statesman, Seneca, insisted that we should be aware of our place in two communities, one local and the other worldwide, believing that we can only understand ourselves in relation to others who think differently. Deep in 16th century rural France, Michel de Montaigne observed in his famous essay *On Educating Children*: 'Frequent commerce with the world can be an astonishing source of light for a man's judgment.' Victor Hugo urged his audiences in 1843, *'avoir pour patrie le monde et pour nation l'humanité'*. (To have as one's homeland the world, and as one's nation, humanity.)

Nor is this a peculiarly western mindset. A century before Diogenes, Confucius wrote, 'One cannot consort with birds and beasts. If I do not associate with humankind, with whom shall I associate?' and much nearer our own times the Nobel laureate, Rabindranath Tagore, who founded an international school in Bengal as early as 1901, wrote proudly of the cosmopolitan influences on his life and was severely criticized for not giving greater support to Indian nationalism.

Humanity, diversity and shared values

The acceptance of a shared humanity, belonging to one human community with a universal understanding of 'joy, fear, sorrow, devotion, valour, rage', lies at the heart of world citizenship. Whatever our differences, we believe they are hugely outweighed by what we all have in common. I have taken that list of qualities from Conrad's novel *Heart of Darkness,* which contains the following description of the Europeans' violent encounter with African tribesmen as they steam slowly up the River Congo:

> It was unearthly, and the men were – No, they were not inhuman. Well, you know, that was the worst of it – the suspicion of their not being inhuman. It would come slowly to one. They howled and leaped, and spun, and made horrid faces; but what thrilled you was just the thought of their humanity – like yours – the thought of your remote kinship with this wild and passionate uproar.

Evidently within the common framework of our shared humanity lies an extraordinary diversity of human behaviour. Learning to live with difference, difference that is so often perceived as threatening, so rarely seen as enriching, is a huge challenge facing the citizen of the world. Agreement that 'other people, with their differences may also be right' (I quote from the mission statement of the IB) is possible only within the supportive framework of a shared set of values. Only if we can agree on the same fundamental commitment to the sanctity of life, to justice, to forgiveness and to basic human rights can we respect what the UK's Chief Rabbi, Jonathan Sacks, has called the 'dignity of difference'.

> The glory of the created world is its astonishing multiplicity: the thousands of different languages spoken by mankind, the hundreds of faiths, the proliferation of cultures, the sheer variety of the imaginative expressions of the human spirit...[1]

For Sacks, 'unity creates diversity'; I am suggesting that it is the unity of universal values that supports diversity. For example:

- the universal value of unrestricted access to educational opportunity means I cannot support a group that would deny it to women.
- the long-term value of reconciliation between conflicting groups means that I can support different cultural interpretations of historic truth.
- the strong commitment to family loyalty in many societies helps me to understand, if not to support, the likelihood of nepotism and corruption.

I have now introduced you to the four main themes of international education:

- cultural understanding;
- our common humanity;
- human diversity; and
- shared values.

My book, *Educating the Global Citizen*, is a selection of lectures, articles and essays exploring each of those themes.[2] You can read more about Montaigne and his struggle in 1580 to reconcile cultural diversity with cannibalism; how Jean Jacques Rousseau proposed a 'social contract' in 1762 to enable diverse groups to live in peace; how Immanuel Kant proposed the creation of a 'league of nations' in 1795 and how Captain Nicolas Baudin's circumnavigation of Tasmania in 1802 sharpened his perception of a common humanity.

World government

I said there was a political dimension to Roosevelt's call for world citizenship, made on 20 January 1945. The President had less than three months to live so he was not present on June 26 when the representatives of 45 nations met in San Francisco to sign the Charter of the United Nations. The first durable foundations of world government had been laid; world citizenship was no longer just a philosophical concept, it had become a political reality. Over the next generation, institutions would be built to promulgate a world view on almost every aspect of our lives: security (UN), migration (IOM), employment (ILO), health (WHO), climate (WMO), trade (WTO), intellectual property (WIPO), and education (UNESCO), to mention some of the best known, but by no means all, of the new breed of international organization.

They have had a mixed record of success. None has been perfect, some have enjoyed much better leadership than others and a few have been subject to deliberate campaigns of vilification but I have not heard of any serious alternatives being proposed. In the sense that individuals now owe their allegiance, in some small degree, to international bodies (like the International Court of Justice) and in part derive their protection from international bodies (like the High Commission for Refugees), we can say that the description 'world citizen' has some practical meaning. But much more compelling is the stark reality of national interdependence and the increasing recognition that the world's major challenges, which include environmental degradation, poverty, disease and terrorism, can only be tackled successfully through international cooperation.

International or global?

It is now time to return to my title because, so far, I have said very little about education. But first I must move the debate into the 21st century. 'The world' which surrounded Confucius and Diogenes means little to us today. Montaigne's world was informed by early reports coming back from the European exploration of the Americas. Victor Hugo was writing just before the 'year of revolutions' (1848), which opened up the first cracks in the great European empires. The world's oldest international school, in Geneva, was the product of the First World War, and the International Baccalaureate and the closely associated United World College movement were founded during the 1960s, the most dangerous decade of the Cold War.

All that is now history. The *globe* (and I deliberately choose that word in preference to the *world*) the globe of which our students are young citizens, has been dramatically changed by the phenomenon known as globalization – the unprecedented movement of capital, goods, services, people, ideas and cultures – and we must start educating young people for today's rather than yesterday's challenges. The far-off international world of frontiers, smallpox vaccination certificates, airmail letter cards, unreliable telephone lines, calm and welcoming airports, exotic food and travel guides belongs to the 20th century when, if we so chose, we could ignore it all and stay at home. In the 21st century globalization is here on our doorsteps. The catch-phrase 'think globally; act locally' contains, like most clichés, an essential truth because it is at home, not at some distant border crossing, that:

- new forms of communication change the nature of our relationships;
- off-shoring and out-sourcing put at risk our jobs;
- the cost of labour in China affects the cost of our house mortgages;
- conflict in the Middle East threatens our daily security; and
- mass migration alters our national identity.

What should the appropriate response of international educators be to the phenomenon of globalization?

- Should we encourage the global expansion of 'one programme fits all'? Could the IB, for example, become the educational equivalent of the global Big Mac? I very much doubt it.
- Shall we see a further polarization into the haves and have-nots, with the benefits of an international education available only to a privileged minority? I very much hope not.
- Can international educators share their experience to the benefit of other systems of education? I very much hope so and it is this path that I intend to follow for the remaining few minutes of this address.

Globalization means managing complexity and difference

My own thinking about the relationship between education and globalization started in 2002 with an invitation from Professor Howard Gardner to participate in a Harvard retreat, at the Pocantico Conference

Centre in Tarrytown, New York. The eventual outcome of this work was the first book that specifically addresses education and globalization.[3] In the opening chapter, its co-editor, Professor Suárez-Orozco, identifies two domains that he believes will challenge schooling worldwide in the 21st century. The first is the domain of **difference**:

> Globalization decisively unmakes the coherence that the modernist project of the nineteenth-and twentieth-century nation state promised to deliver – the neat fit between territory, language and identity... Managing **difference** is becoming one of the greatest challenges to multicultural countries.

The second is the domain of **complexity**:

> Globalization engenders **complexity**. Throughout the world it is generating more intricate demographic profiles, economic realities, political processes, technology and media, cultural facts and artifacts and identities.

Globalization means understanding people on their terms

The second source that has informed my own thinking is Howard Gardner's latest book, *Five Minds for the Future*. Without five very different minds, argues Gardner, we shall be at the mercy of forces that we can't understand, let alone control. Given the nature of his earlier work, four of the five are unsurprising: the disciplined, synthesizing, creating and ethical minds. But the fifth is unexpected, the **respectful** mind, and I want to quote a key extract:

> ...I must try to understand other persons on their own terms, make an imaginative leap when necessary to convey my trust in them, and try so far as possible to make common cause with them and to be worthy of their trust. This stance does not mean that I ignore my own beliefs, nor that I necessarily accept or pardon all that I encounter.... But I am obliged to make the effort, and not merely to assume that what I had once believed on the basis of scattered impressions is necessarily true. Such humility may, in turn, engender positive responses in others.[4]

Globalization means increased competition

My third source of stimulus has been Thomas Friedman's best seller, *The Earth is Flat*. This is an entertaining and hard-hitting account of the way globalization has allowed new players like India and China to compete economically with the developed world on a more level playing field. Here is a typical quote:

> Jobs are going to go where the best educated work force is with the most competitive infrastructure and environment for creativity and supportive government.[5]

Friedman concludes that it will not be the United States where, indeed, the real income of the median American family is already lower than it was five years ago.

Acknowledging my debt to these sources, I am going to identify three educational approaches, which I believe will help to prepare young people for a globalized world.

The historical context of globalization

The first is relatively straightforward and uncontroversial. Globalization is not a new phenomenon. Arguably, we are witnessing at least its fourth cycle. The first was launched in 1492 from Portugal, produced the first trans-Atlantic trading system and a century or so later had caused the deaths of more than 90% of the original inhabitants of the Americas. The second cycle, two hundred years later, saw nine million Africans shipped to the Americas where they made good the labour shortages caused by the first cycle. In the UK we have recently acknowledged this shameful episode in our history with events commemorating the bicentenary of the Act of Parliament that led to the abolition of slavery. The third cycle of globalization began with the huge growth of imperial trade in the 19th century and mass migration from Europe to North America. The current cycle started with the liberalization of international trade after the Second World War and has been driven at an increasingly frantic pace by new processes of information and communication technology.

Each cycle of globalization has seen significant increases in human productivity. In most cases these have trickled down to improve overall standards of living relative to countries untouched by the process. But short-term benefits have often gone to tiny minorities and have usually been achieved at the expense of acute suffering over many generations. Those who were asked to wait for benefits in the long run might have recalled the comment of economist, John Maynard Keynes: 'In the long run, we're all dead.'

There are parallels to be drawn here and contrasts to be made. For slaves and sugar, could we substitute oil and armaments or (dare I say it in Hong Kong?) China tea and Indian opium? There is evidence to be sifted and alternative explanations to be weighed. There are issues to be argued about and some lessons to be learned. All this speaks to me of a good history lesson and I would like to see globalization included in history syllabuses as a thematic topic. I note for example the following themes in the IB Diploma history course:

- the causes, practices and effects of war;
- the rise and rule of independent states; and
- religion and minorities.

And wonder why 'cycles of globalization' is not among them. We should acknowledge that globalization is a defining movement, shaping the development of humankind. We should also acknowledge that, like other cycles, it will run its course. Open markets rule today ... but tomorrow?

Responding to winners and losers

My second theme is more complex; indeed it is complexity itself, which, you will remember, was identified by the Harvard group as one of the major challenges facing education in the 21st century. With globalization:

- more information is more available more quickly;
- more people are claiming a right, and indeed are able, to participate;
- paradoxically, perhaps, more emphasis is being given to ethical issues;
- values which once represented ageless standards have become more relative;
- possible solutions are more likely to be presented from multiple viewpoints; and
- we are more reluctant to trust authority, feeling more empowered ourselves.

How can education best respond to this growing complexity? **First**, I believe, by insisting that students study a range of different disciplines that, for example, help them to grasp the scientific, statistical and economic aspects of a carbon credit scheme or the historical, cultural and political aspects of the Iraq conflict. In other words, a broad curriculum. **Second**, by learning about the status of different forms of knowledge and thereby developing a sense of intellectual honesty. This is why I believe the IB's Theory of Knowledge course is so important – here is a typical ToK question:

> What are the differences between 'I am certain' and 'it is certain' and is passionate conviction ever sufficient for justifying knowledge?

Third, by exploring some aspect of globalization in depth, bringing to bear learning from different disciplines. The appropriate balance between breadth and depth is never easy to achieve in the school curriculum but my favourite description of the IB Diploma is: 'the programme that had the courage to leave some gaps.'

In a word, the global citizen needs to be smart, to carry around a well-used toolkit of critical thinking skills. But that is no longer enough. Any serious response to globalization must be honest about its winners and losers. In China and India, for example, which have had the necessary education and technology to participate in the globalization movement, hundreds of millions of people have been moved out of poverty. The World Bank reported that roughly 375m Chinese were living in acute poverty (less than US$1 per day) in 1990; the figure decreased to 212m in 2001 and, if current trends are maintained, will decrease further to about 16m by 2015. In complete contrast, the comparable figures in sub-Saharan Africa increase from 227m to 313m to 340m. Seventy percent of people in the developing world depend directly or indirectly upon agriculture, and the massive agricultural subsidies in the North depress the incomes of those in the South. The average cow in Europe receives a subsidy of about US$2 a day while 40% of those in the developing world have less than that amount to live on.

From all the many powerful passages in Friedman's book, the one that has stuck with me is his description of the social entrepreneur. What we need, he says, are people who 'combine a business school brain with a social worker's heart'. Smartness, yes, but smartness linked to compassion, and compassion means pity combined with a desire to help.

Where is the other person coming from?

And that leads me to my third theme of globalization – difference – which I reintroduce with that comment from Howard Gardner: 'I must try to understand other persons on their own terms.' If you accept that globalization is bringing very different people more closely together (the phrase 'global village' is commonly used) then the ability to understand 'where the other person is coming from' becomes of paramount importance. Simply walking away from those you do not understand, or disagree with, is no longer an option.

So, for example, speaking the other person's language immediately puts them, not you, in the stronger position of whatever exchange is taking place. It is a way you can pay homage to their culture.

> Learning a language – somebody else's language – is a kind gesture. It's a gesture of interest. It really is a fundamental way to reach out to somebody and say, "I care about you. I want you to know that I am interested in not only how you talk but how you live."

That quote comes from an unlikely source, President George W Bush addressing US university principals in 2006, but it nonetheless expresses a very powerful sentiment.

Working on a common project with people of different cultural backgrounds is another way of learning more about their mind-set, which is why community service is so important, not so much for the service rendered as for the lessons learned in rendering it.

But I want to end by highlighting an issue that has worried me since I became involved with international education. I have no convincing answer but I want to share the problem because, in Hong Kong, you could be well placed to offer some suggestions. A moment ago I referred to the smart global citizen carrying around a toolkit of critical thinking skills because (I quote Suárez-Orozco again) 'cognitive flexibility and agility will win the day'. But it is my experience that people from many cultures are not noticeably flexible and agile when it comes to cognitive reasoning: their minds seem to run along different lines. Here, again, is the Indian Nobel laureate, Rabindranath Tagore:

> What I object to is the artificial arrangement by which this foreign education tends to occupy all the space of our national mind and thus kills, or hampers, the great opportunity for the creation of new thought by a new combination of truths.

Yet those of us working in the field of international education have never seemed very interested in 'the great opportunity for the creation of new thought by a new combination of truths', nor especially concerned that, for example, the International Baccalaureate is not really international at all, but constructed entirely upon a western humanist view of learning.

I remember being impressed by the emphasis given by the American psychologist, Jerome Bruner, to intuitive thinking:

> The complementary nature of intuitive and analytic thinking should, we think, be recognized. Through intuitive thinking the individual may often arrive at solutions to problems which he would not achieve at all, or at best more slowly, through analytic thinking... Unfortunately, the formalism of school learning has somehow devalued intuition.

I remember, too, the distinction made by Bruner between logical-scientific thinking and narrative thinking and his observation that most schools treat the arts of narrative – song, drama, fiction, theatre – as decorative rather than necessary, at best as leisure pursuits.

I remember listening to a fascinating presentation by a group of students in Accra, Ghana, about the extensive use of proverbs in their teaching.

I remember the experience I had at the International School of Geneva of frequent clashes between the Cartesian logic of the Francophone teachers and the empirical pragmatism of the Anglophones. How rarely was this ever used to the students' advantage; instead it was seen as a confusing nuisance.

I remember the research that shows how some cultures emphasize the group rather than the individual in their learning; how some are prepared to take more risks than others in the formulation of hypotheses.

But none of these 'I remembers' adds up to a convincing response to Tagore's search for the 'creation of new thought by a new combination of truths' and I think this is one of the biggest failures of international education. 'Cognitive flexibility and agility' may indeed win the day in a competitive world driven by market forces but the time will surely come when we shall want to give proper recognition to the contribution to be made to the quality of our lives by alternative modes of thinking.

The IB has schools in 125 different countries yet during my six years as director general I cannot remember asking any one of them for advice and practical proposals in this area. Nor can I remember any one of them volunteering.

Summary

We have covered a lot of ground and it is time to sum up. We started by looking at the philosophical and the political dimensions of world citizenship.

In doing so we arrived at the four basic tenets of international education: cultural understanding, our common humanity, diversity and shared values. I believe these are timeless but they require reinterpretation in the context of the real world.

This led me to make a distinction between the world issues of the past and global issues of the present.

We went on to examine three ways in which international educators could respond to this new challenge: a study of globalization in its historic context, skills for dealing with complexity and learning to understand better the other person's point of view.

From this I identified an issue that I believe deserves greater recognition and study – culturally different modes of thought.

Let me end with the complete Victor Hugo quote. It is poignant that an IB colleague first saw it pinned to the wall of an African IB school in Togo.

> *Un jour, espérons-le. Le globe sera civilisé. Tous les points de la demeure humaine seront éclairés et alors sera accompli le magnifique rêve de l'intelligence: avoir pour patrie le Monde et pour nation l'Humanité.*
>
> One day, we hope, the world will be civilized. All points of this human abode will be enlightened and then the magnificent dream of intelligent life will have been achieved: to have as one's homeland the World, and as one's nation, Humanity.

Bibliography
1. Sacks, J. (2002): *The Dignity of Difference; how to avoid the clash of civilizations.* London: Continuum
2. Walker, G. (2006): *Educating the Global Citizen.* Great Glemham: John Catt Educational.
3. Suárez-Orozco, M. & Qin-Hilliard, D., eds (2004): *Globalization; culture and education in the new millennium.* Berkeley, CA: University of California Press.
4. Gardner, H. (2006): *Five Minds for the Future.* Boston, MA: Harvard Business School Press.
5. Friedman, T. (2005): *The World is Flat.* London: Allen Lane.

Review of *Five Minds for the Future*

by Howard Gardner

Boston, MA: Harvard Business School Press, 2006

Don't be fooled by the informal, almost conversational, tone. For the first time in a long line of distinguished books, Howard Gardner is not telling us what is, not even what might be; he is telling us what should be. There is a political dimension to this book, starting with his actual choice of five minds (others might have included a religious mind, for example, or a democratic mind) and it is reinforced with key quotations from two political giants, Benjamin Franklin, 'We must indeed all hang together, or, most assuredly we shall all hang separately', and Winston Churchill, 'The empires of the future will be empires of the mind'.

Formal education is conservative, says Gardner, which is not necessarily a bad thing. But it is doomed never to be quite fit for purpose, always lagging behind the times, never adapting fast enough. Adapting to science/technology and to the phenomenon of globalization are the current challenges. The first is hardly new: writing almost a century ago in his powerful political novel, *The New Machiavelli*, H G Wells (1911) articulates his concern for the suffocating study of Latin and Greek:

> We came out into the new world no teacher has yet had the power and courage to grasp and expound. Life and death sang all about one, joys and fears on such a scale, in such an intricacy as never Greek nor Roman knew.[1]

But even Wells would have marvelled at the way information technology is now transforming our lives with equal measures of joy and fear, providing the main driving force behind the latest – because it is by no means the first – cycle of globalization. The definition I like best is: 'The widening, deepening and speeding up of world-wide interconnectedness in all aspects of contemporary social life.'[2] And this time globalization really is different in terms of its breadth, depth and speed of penetration so it is astonishing that so very little has been written about its implications for education.[3] This is the huge question that Gardner is addressing when he argues that 'our survival as a planet may depend on the cultivation of this pentad of mental dispositions' – a pentad of five minds: disciplined, synthesizing, creating, respectful and ethical.

Undisciplined students, insists Gardner, 'are essentially stranded in the same intellectual place as barbarians' because they have no idea how to master bodies of knowledge and key procedures. He reckons it takes about a decade to acquire a systematic mastery of the distinctive ways of thinking about the world, which he takes to mean science, mathematics, history and at least one art form. The **disciplined mind** is not measured by how much you have learned, but by your ability to use that knowledge in unfamiliar situations and this is where even the most prestigious systems of education have consistently been found wanting.

Individuals bereft of disciplinary understanding: '...are then completely dependent upon others when they must take decisions about their own health or welfare or vote on issues of importance for their time.' I am reminded of C P Snow's influential lecture, *The Two Cultures and the Scientific Revolution*,[4] in which he highlighted the need for those who shape important political decisions to feel equally at ease on either side of the arts/science divide, enabling them to cross with confidence the disciplinary 'Snow line'. We seem to have made little progress in that direction in the intervening half century.

Thus far we have been on rather familiar Gardner territory[5] but he now introduces the **synthesizing mind**, which confers the ability 'to knit together information from disparate sources into a coherent whole'. The rate of growth of knowledge has become explosive and Gardner selects Matthew Arnold as perhaps the last individual who could be said to have 'known everything worth knowing'. My choice would be Benjamin Jowett, Victorian Master of Balliol College, Oxford, who (according to a literary pupil) offered a much neater solution:

> First come I. My name is Jowett.
> There's no knowledge but I know it.
> I am the Master of this College.
> What I don't know isn't knowledge.

But you can't get away with that any more and, in the 21st century, Gardner tells us that we need both those with laser minds who can penetrate into the deepest recesses of a discipline, and others with a searchlight intelligence who will more readily perceive connections across disciplines.

Some important scientific searchlights – Eddington,[6] Bronowski[7] and Dawkins,[8] for example – come readily to mind but let us not forget Clark's remarkable study of civilization[9] and Wells's ambitious outline of history.[10]

There is an important political significance to this kind of work because synthesizers bring access and therefore legitimacy to complex disciplines; they build platforms of public understanding from which more detailed, and sometimes more controversial, explorations can be authorized – genetic engineering offers a good example. Synthesis is an ambitious activity and synthesizers will often get it wrong: I doubt whether H G Wells's sweeping summaries (modestly described as being 'a plain history of life and mankind') would impress many academic historians today. Synthesis must therefore go hand in hand with analysis, breaking the whole back into its observable parts, or some very strange and dangerous conclusions may be reached.

And this brings us to the chapter on the **creating mind**, which I found just a little dull and predictable (Gardner admits rather wearily at the outset that, as a researcher in psychology, the most routine question from audiences is how to nurture creativity) but it is nonetheless enlivened by an instructive example of creating gone awry – the case of cold fusion. In 1989 two scientists from the University of Utah took their creative thinking several steps beyond their discipline, when they claimed to have carried out a process of sustained nuclear fusion at room temperature in a conventional laboratory. The whole world marvelled – for a couple of days – at such an elegant solution to the world's energy problems. Alas the scientists had got it wrong and their work proved to be ill-disciplined, ignoring many of the criteria that maintain the credibility of scientific research: peer review, reproducibility, meticulous reporting and a rational explanation that links the new to the old. 'Only through the honing of discipline would genuinely creative options ultimately emerge' warns Gardner, and it is a timely warning because our struggle to get to grips with increasingly complex issues will be threatened by all kinds of politically motivated snake-oil peddlers.

And so to the **respectful mind** where Gardner breaks – for him – new ground. Can he offer new perspectives to international educators on what – for them – is rather familiar ground? Does he help us, for example, to understand better one of the four UNESCO[11] pillars for education for the 21st century: 'learning to live with others?' For Gardner, respect, rather than love, for others is a reasonable goal:

> Rather than ignoring differences, being inflamed by them, or seeking to annihilate them through love or hate, I call upon human beings to accept the differences, learn to live with them and value those who belong to other cohorts.

Well, yes, but what practical steps can be taken to educate young people to accept, learn to live with and value those differences? Let us try to put our first three minds to it...

I think we could adopt a **disciplined** approach to the challenge of learning to live with others, invoking key concepts such as the significance of culture, our understanding of emotional intelligence and criteria for truth derived from the Universal Declaration of Human Rights. Then there are plenty of **synthesizing** minds that are describing our accumulated knowledge of how to get on with other people in a variety of different forms: academic research, outstanding contemporary novels, different art forms and individuals whose lives have been an inspiration. Finally, there is unlimited scope for **creating** new pathways. Gardner, for example, quotes Daniel Barenboim and his inspirational West-Eastern Divan orchestra. I can quote the United World College-International Baccalaureate project in Bosnia and Herzegovina, which offers a new model for post-conflict education and most readers of this review will have their own examples of creative thinking about learning to live with others. So there we are: quite quickly we have begun to imagine the first steps of a formal programme to help young people to develop a respectful mind.

The description of the **ethical mind** brings Gardner back into familiar surroundings[12] and it opens with a reminder of the importance of 'good work': good in the triple sense of quality, responsibility and meaning; work in the sense of contribution to society – 'a commitment to work towards the realization of a virtuous community'. Influence, for good or evil, comes vertically from parents, other adult models and mentors; horizontally, it comes from peers and colleagues. A good worker has a consistent set of principles, is transparent and maintains those principles even when they threaten self-interest.

> As disciplined learners, it is our job to understand the world. But if we are to be ethical human beings, it is equally our job to use that understanding to improve the quality of life and living and to bear witness when that understanding (or misunderstanding) is being used in destructive ways.

Sadly, as Gardner knows from his own research, the temptation amongst young ambitious people to bend or break the ethical rules is often overwhelming and when cheats prosper, the robust principle of enlightened self-interest begins to break down. While no society explicitly 'endorses falsehood, dishonesty, disloyalty, gross inequity', many suffer from endemic corruption and his examples of Enron and Arthur Andersen remind us that they are not all located in banana republics.

This is an ambitious book. No doubt some will argue that Gardner has tried to build too much upon too insubstantial a foundation of research, but that misses the point; in fact it misses two points. First, a reading of his earlier work will supply much of the more detailed evidence and second, this was never intended to be an academic thesis. *Five Minds For The Future* is aimed at a much wider audience:

> It is up to the education system as a whole – the education system in its broadest sense – to ensure that the ensemble of minds is cultivated... When I speak of the "broadest sense" of education, I have in mind that schools alone cannot do the job.

Indeed they cannot and that is why the book must be read far beyond institutions of formal education. If 21st century teachers are expected to be pedagogues (disciplined mind), 'knowledge artists' (synthesizing mind), risk-takers (creating mind), mentors (respectful mind) and role models (ethical mind) they will need the active support and participation of the widest possible community. *Five Minds* is a manifesto, a public declaration about education as it should be.

References

1. Wells, H. (1911): *The New Machiavelli*. London: The Bodley Head.
2. Held, D. et al (1999): *Global Transformations: politics, economics and culture*. Cambridge: Polity Press
3. Suárez-Orozco, M. and Qin-Hilliard, D. (2004): *Globalization: culture and education in the new millennium*. Berkeley, CA: University of California Press.
4. Snow, C. (1959): *The Two Cultures and the Scientific Revolution. The Rede Lecture*. Cambridge: Cambridge University Press.
5. Gardner, H. (1991): *The Unschooled Mind*. New York: Basic Books; Gardner, H. (1999): *The Disciplined Mind*. New York: Simon and Schuster.
6. Eddington, A. (1928): *The Nature of the Physical World*. Cambridge: Cambridge University Press.
7. Bronowski, J. (1974): *The Ascent of Man*. London: BBC.
8. Dawkins, R. (1976): *The Selfish Gene*. Oxford: Oxford University Press.
9. Clark, K. (1970): *Civilisation*. London: BBC.
10. Wells, H. (1931): *The Outline of History*. New York: Garden City Publishing Co.
11. UNESCO (1996): *Learning: the treasure within*. Paris: UNESCO.
12. Gardner, H., Csikszentmihalyi, M. and Damon, W. (2001): *Good Work*. New York: Basic Books.

Education: for the Nation or for the World?

Chautauqua Institution, New York

4 July 2006

Chapter 1: Defining national frontiers

When Tony Blair's Labour Party came to power in the United Kingdom in 1997, the new Prime Minister was asked to list his government's priorities. We have just three, he said, famously – education, education and education. In saying that, Blair was not thinking of his country's responsibilities as a partner in the European Union, or a founder member of the Commonwealth, or a permanent member of the security council of the United Nations. He was thinking of the domestic needs of the United Kingdom for which his government had just become responsible. Education, like charity, begins at home.

This is confirmed by recent history. During the 1920s, the newly founded League of Nations, meeting in Geneva, frequently debated the role of education in its struggle to avoid renewed global conflict. Nonetheless, the League consistently refused to accept any formal responsibility for it. Its delegates argued that education was a national responsibility with which the League had no right to interfere. Instead, it set up an Intellectual Cooperation Committee (ICC), which included such eminent personalities as Marie Curie, Albert Einstein, Bela Bartok and Thomas Mann, but it refused to provide a budget to allow it to remain in Geneva.

The ICC therefore moved to Paris and in 1946 it provided the seed for the growth of the United Nations Educational, Scientific and Cultural Organisation (UNESCO). I shall return to UNESCO in a moment, because it has a part to play in my story, but for the moment I am making the point that education has always been a national priority. Indeed, in our increasingly globalized 21st century, education is one of the few remaining independent levers that governments believe they can pull in order to influence national economic and social policy.

For the past 150 years then, education has been linked to a national purpose. In my own country the priority in the 19th century was the education of a newly franchised population to cast its votes responsibly; in your country,

Horace Mann, the first Secretary of the Massachusetts Board of Education, saw education as the most effective means to reduce poverty. More recently, when Singapore was created in 1965 its government quite deliberately designed a style of education that would help to shape a new national identity. African countries gaining independence in the 1960s and seventies used education as a means of re-shaping their national identity and casting aside the influence of the colonial power.

However, the biggest national driver has been economic and the proven link between the quality of education and per capita Gross Domestic Product (GDP). In a recent report the World Bank insisted that it was the acquisition of skills, particularly literacy, that measured GDP increases rather than the length of the educational process but, whatever the detail, no government dares ignore the broad relationship between education and economic prosperity. No wonder, then, that developed nations examine the outcomes of the PISA exercise (Programme of International Student Assessment, administered by OECD and involving nearly 40 different countries) very carefully indeed and ask, yet again, what is the secret of Finland's success?

Former US Education Secretary, Rod Paige, commented in 2004:

> The PISA results are a blinking warning light...

But he was only echoing a much more dramatic warning contained in the 1983 report of the National Commission on Excellence in Education (A Nation at Risk):

> If an unfriendly foreign power had attempted to impose on America the mediocre educational performance that exists today, we might well have viewed it as an act of war.

The economic imperative is important and Thomas Friedman in his best-selling book, *The World is Flat*, has become the latest Cassandra, linking the impending decline of the United States to its inadequate system of public education.

But a more powerful argument still for education remaining a national responsibility is its central role in the transmission of culture from one generation to the next. Decisions about who should teach, what they should teach and how they should teach it lie at the heart of cultural transmission. Whose view of the nation's future needs? Which selected elements of the nation's culture? What style of learning? These questions have occupied the greatest minds and have provided some of the most inspiring statements about education and learning. It is at this point that education becomes worth studying!

For example, just a few weeks before he died in 1854, Horace Mann said to an audience of students that:

> You should be ashamed to die until you have won some victory for humanity.

The distinguished English poet and critic, Matthew Arnold, (who visited the United States twice in the 1880s), was a powerful supporter of state education and he argued that it should:

> ...make the best that has been thought and known in the world current everywhere; to make all men live in an atmosphere of sweetness and light, where they may use ideas ... freely – nourished and not bound by them.

That was 1869 and John Dewey, exactly 30 years later, was saying the same thing in less flowery language in his famous assertion:

> What the best and wisest parent wants for his own child, that must the community want for all of its children. Any other ideal for our schools is narrow and unlovely; acted upon it destroys our democracy.

So, let me sum up this opening chapter of my lecture by saying that education has always been perceived as a national responsibility - more than that, as a national priority. This has been not only for pragmatic reasons, in particular to sustain economic growth, but also because education has been the means of defining, debating and maintaining a nation's culture and therefore its very sense of identity.

Anyone who believes that education has little effect and that it all comes to the same thing in the end should read the classic study of the 1970s by the Cornell psychologist, Urie Bronfenbrenner, entitled *Two Worlds of Childhood*, in which he examines the hugely different experiences of childhood in America and the Soviet Union. Incidentally, Bronfenbrenner looks for a criterion for judging the worth of a society that goes beyond GDP, crime rates or health statistics and he proposes: 'the concern of one generation for the next.' I think I may come back to that in a moment.

Chapter 2: Thinking across frontiers

There have, however, always been those whose intellectual curiosity and breadth of vision have carried them across the frontiers of their own nation.

Challenges from a New World

The French essayist, Montaigne, wrote in 1580:

> Mixing with the world has a marvellously clarifying effect on a man's judgement. We are all confined and pent up within ourselves, and our sight has contracted to the length of our noses.

When someone asked Socrates of what country he was he did not reply 'of Athens', but 'of the world':

> This great world, which some still reckon to be but one example of a whole genus, is the mirror into which we must look if we are to behold ourselves from the proper standpoint.

A similar view had been developed by the Ancient Greeks and it was indeed the sceptic, Diogenes, who first used the term 'cosmopolitan', meaning a citizen of the world. Five centuries later, the Roman statesman, Seneca, insisted that education must develop within us a sense of belonging both to a world community and to the community of our birth.

Now, when Socrates, Diogenes, Seneca and even 16th century Montaigne speak of 'the world' we need to be careful, because their world is very different from the one we perceive today. Nonetheless, their essential message remains unchanged over two and a half millennia, namely we understand ourselves better in relation to other people who think and behave differently to ourselves. We were created to be part of diversity.

This concept of what we might now call 'global citizenship' is not without its critics, particularly here in the United States. For example, the Director of EdWatch, based in Minnesota, is quoted as saying she opposes the International Baccalaureate Diploma Programme on ideological grounds because it teaches 'a sense of global citizenship which is contrary to what it is to be an American citizen'.

Now, it is not clear whether she believes that *all* interpretations of global citizenship are at odds with what it is to be an American citizen, or just the IB's particular version, but I strongly suspect it is the former. She, and many others in the United States, perhaps fearful of some historically dubious champions of cosmopolitanism, believe that the two simply cannot co-exist. Well, that is a reassuring and uncomplicated view. Alas, real life is rather more complex and I have chosen three examples to illustrate that complexity.

A few years ago I was taken to task in the press by another American lady, this time living on Long Island. She accused me of admiring the Geneva philosopher, Jean-Jacques Rousseau – and to avoid any misunderstanding on this point let me enter an immediate plea of 'guilty as charged'. My critic pointed out that Rousseau had ambiguous views on national sovereignty, on religion and on the ownership of property. She is right: Rousseau had ambiguous views on most important issues, which is what makes him so completely human and so totally fascinating to read.

In *The Social Contract*, for example, Rousseau suggests that, in the interests of achieving greater corporate security, countries should be prepared to surrender some of their individual autonomy. This proposal upset not only my Long Island critic, but also the Genevois authorities and in 1762 they stripped him of his citizenship of which he was so proud (the original manuscript is signed *Citoyen de Genève*). The bus I used to take to work in Geneva went right past the site of Rousseau's birthplace and engraved on the wall I read each day his famous memory of his father:

> *Mon père, en m'embrassant, fut saisi d'un tressaillement que je crois sentir et partager encore. Jean-Jacques, me disait-il, aime ton pays.*
>
> My father would embrace me and shudder in a way that I can still feel and share. Jean-Jacques, he said, love your country.

But Jean-Jacques was forced to flee from his beloved country, to seek exile in Switzerland (remember Geneva was still an independent republic), then in England and finally in France where he died. Small wonder, then, that Rousseau's views on national sovereignty are ambiguous!

Next time you are in London, near Trafalgar Square, go and look at the statue of Edith Cavell opposite the church of St Martin in the Fields. In 1915, Edith Cavell was matron of a hospital in German-occupied Brussels from where she used her influence to smuggle dozens of British soldiers back to the neutral safety of the Netherlands. She was found out, tried, found guilty and shot at dawn. Her execution was a propaganda disaster for the German government because, predictably, she became a martyr overnight. Here was a true patriot.

However, the full story is not that simple because Edith Cavell was working for the Red Cross and her covert actions had violated the strict rules of neutrality to which all Red Cross workers are bound. She had decided that national patriotism should take priority over international convention but the British Government thought otherwise and did little to help her. There it would have remained, a rather sad national-international dilemma, if she had not spoken to her chaplain just before her execution the famous words that are engraved on her memorial:

> I realise that patriotism is not enough. I must have no hatred or bitterness towards anyone.

Words that would make a fitting motto for the Red Cross and Red Crescent.

My third example comes closer to home, that is to say to the International Baccalaureate (IB). Any list of founders of international education and the closely associated United World College movement and the IB, would certainly include the name of Kurt Hahn. Hahn was Jewish and helped to found Salem School in Germany which is today an IB school. In 1933, after being arrested by the Nazis, he fled to Britain where he founded Gordonstoun School, launched the Outward Bound movement and was hugely influential in the creation of the Duke of Edinburgh's Award Scheme. In the 1950s he was a key member of the group that founded Atlantic College, the first of the United World Colleges.

Hahn's message was simple:

> There will be no indoctrination – but through the bond of active humanity a brotherhood will find itself alive to the common purpose.

However, the motivation that lay behind the foundation of Atlantic College was not quite so straightforward. In 1957, Hahn wrote:

> The North Atlantic Powers have built up a formidable alliance (NATO) to deter aggression. To succeed in their purpose they must instil into the citizens of the 15 Member Nations a sense of unity and resolution sufficient to inspire them to work positively for peace as well as defensively against the threat of war... The enemies of the West cannot fail to appreciate that, as soon as they can lull their victims into a false sense of security, old discords will break out again and will cripple the potentiality of the Alliance for concerted action... We want to submit a plan to build western solidarity on a more reliable basis than fear: namely on the resolution of young people, strong in their belief in the common cause of the free world...

These are not exactly the politically correct words of a global citizen, and they even resonate with recent statements coming from the White House on the spread of western values linked to the concept of democracy. I do not quote them in order to cast doubt on Kurt Hahn's international credentials; someone who knew him well described his patriotism as starting with a concern for a service to the local community, spreading out to one's own country and ending in 'tender love of all mankind'. No: I have chosen Hahn, Cavell and Rousseau, to show how there is usually an overlapping of thought and action when one tries to distinguish the national from the international; we have to learn to live with both. You will all have heard the expression, 'think globally and act locally'.

In summary, therefore, of this second chapter, I have tried to show that there have always been people ready to think beyond national frontiers in order to imagine things from a different perspective. That does not require anyone to surrender their national identity and culture, but rather to take notice of the identity and culture of others. My message this morning is that that this is no longer an intellectual whim for a minority, but a practical necessity for us all.

Chapter 3: Education across frontiers

Am I on my own? Well, a number of messages coming from US administrations in recent years suggest not.

In 2000, the then Secretary of Education, Richard Riley, said:

> I strongly believe that the growth of democracy, economic prosperity and economic stability throughout the world is linked to the advance of education. This is one of the reasons why the United States should have an active and strong international education agenda.

His successor, in the new Republican administration, Rod Paige, making specific reference to the events of September 11 2001, and noting that an astonishing 83% of young Americans surveyed by the *National Geographic* could not find Afghanistan on a map, said:

> No longer can we afford to focus only on the domestic. Our view must turn more outward towards the world, nurturing relationships with other countries and improving international studies in our schools.

> I am directing that we do a better job of exposing our students in this country to other languages, cultures, and challenges outside our borders.

Paige's successor, Margaret Spellings, addressed the US University Presidents Summit on International Education in January of this year:

> The world is changing at a rapid pace, and many of our students lack the skills to succeed in the global knowledge economy... This is not just an education issue; it's an economic issue, a civic issue, a social issue, a national security issue, and it's everybody's issue.

And President Bush, at the same conference, developed this theme

> This initiative is a broad-gauged initiative that deals with the defence of the country, the diplomacy of the country, the intelligence to defend our country and the education of our people.

But then, quite unexpectedly, the President said something which transforms the entire debate and, in a way, becomes the pivot which tips the balance of my lecture. He said:

> Learning a language – somebody else's language – is a kind gesture. It's a gesture of interest. It really is a fundamental way to reach out to somebody and say, 'I care about you. I want you to know that I am interested in not only how you talk but how you live.'

Quite suddenly, our attention is no longer focused on economics and international diplomacy, not even on democracy and the defence of the country. It has gone much deeper: the fundamental challenge is to understand how other people communicate and how other people live their lives. We are beginning to hear the language of global citizenship.

In that statement, President Bush has associated himself with Charles Dickens, who supported a scheme to establish a consortium of international schools throughout Europe in the 1860s, insisting that such schools would encourage:

> ...the tolerance that comes of near acquaintance with different ways of thought.

And with the Indian poet and Nobel laureate, Rabindranath Tagore, who founded an international school in India in 1921 based on a similar philosophy. Tagore wrote:

> When races come together, as in the present age, it should not be merely the gathering of a crowd; there must be a bond of relation or they will collide with each other...

This growing movement of what we might call 'education across frontiers' established its first enduring roots in 1924 when the International School of Geneva was founded to educate the children of the staff of the League of Nations. We have already seen how the League declined any formal responsibility for education, but a group of its staff was quick to launch a school that would encourage, in its diverse students, the same values that the League was trying to instil in its diverse member nations. Today, Ecolint, as it is known across the world, educates some 3500 students on the basis that:

> The activity of the school in all fields and especially in the field of pedagogy shall be based on the principles of equality and solidarity among all peoples and of the equal value of all human beings without the distinction of nationality, race, sex, language or religion.

This movement of – let us now use the accepted name of international education – gathered momentum after the Second World War and in 1946 the United Nations Educational, Scientific and Cultural Organization was established with the inspirational introduction to its constitution, attributed to the American poet, Archibald Macleish:

> Since wars begin in the minds of men, it is in the minds of men that the defences of peace must be constructed.

I said I would return to UNESCO and I do so because, in 1974, its General Conference adopted a recommendation urging all member states to reflect the following guiding principles in the design of their national programmes of education:

- an international dimension and a global perspective in education at all levels and in all its forms;
- understanding and respect for all peoples, their cultures, civilizations, values and ways of life, including domestic ethnic cultures and cultures of other nations;
- awareness of the increasing global interdependence between peoples and nations;
- abilities to communicate with others;
- awareness not only of the rights but also of the duties incumbent upon all individuals, social groups and nations towards each other;
- understanding of the necessity for international solidarity and cooperation; and
- readiness on the part of the individual to participate in solving the problems of his community, his country and the world at large.

Twenty years later, in 1994, these principles, which build a bridge between education for the nation and education for the world, were accepted by the world's ministers of education who were meeting in Geneva. So let us be clear what this means. Every country that is a member of UNESCO has agreed to build an international dimension into its national programmes of education. We should remind ourselves that, not only is your country and mine a member state of UNESCO, but also that its Assistant Director-General for Education is Peter Smith, former State Senator and Lieutenant Governor of Vermont. When asked why he accepted the post, he replied:

> It's simple. I wanted to join the global crusade for human opportunity through quality education and move it towards success.

To summarise my third chapter: for the past 150 years there has been a growing movement of international education that is concerned with understanding people from different cultures, not just as economic competitors or potential threats to our security, but as fellow human beings with the same rights as we have to live peaceful and fulfilled lives on this planet. International education recognizes diversity as a cause for celebration; it also recognizes our common humanity as the basis for sharing the planet's resources. Today, at the beginning of the 21st century, globalization makes it meaningless to speak of 'my world' and 'their world'. We are all living together in 'our world' and our education must reflect that reality.

Chapter 4: Schools across frontiers

A moment ago I spoke about introducing 'an international dimension to national programmes of education'. But what does that actually mean in practice? What am I suggesting schools should be doing differently next Monday morning?

Well already, I imagine, good schools are encouraging their students to think creatively and not merely to regurgitate undigested information; already they are challenging their students to solve problems that require the application of more than one knowledge discipline; already they are devising learning tasks that require cooperation, collaboration and teamwork; and they are creating opportunities to use different modes of communication, including a foreign language.

Let us – optimistically, perhaps – take all that for granted. I believe there are two important additional requirements: a study of globalization itself and a raising of cultural awareness. I do not have time to explore either in detail so let me make just two broad points.

I understand the term 'globalization' to mean more than the movement of different forms of capital around the world; more than the rapid transfer of information. I understand it to embrace those activities that can only be studied meaningfully from a global, rather than a national, perspective. So, for me, 'globalization' includes the steady environmental degradation of our planet, it includes the management of disease, it includes human migration and it includes a knowledge of and respect for the organizations (WHO, IOM, ILO and WMO, for example) that are trying to manage the impact of globalization, particularly on those people who are least able to manage it themselves. And let me remind you that it was the vision and drive of two American presidents, in 1919 and again in 1945, that created first the League and then the United Nations, which led to all those UN-related organizations.

Concerning cultural awareness, I would make just one point. If I am to respect another person's culture then I must start by understanding and respecting my own; its rituals, symbols and heroes; the importance of a shared language and of a shared religion. I can only make sense of my everyday life through a shared cultural identity with those around me. I was reminded recently of the complexity of this subject while reading Toni Morrison's novel, *The Bluest Eye*. Eleven-year-old Pecola, abused by her father, is desperate to acquire the blue eyes of a white child because, for her, they represent true beauty, in contrast, she is convinced, to her own racially-determined ugliness. How can Pecola be helped to understand and respect her own culture? What sort of view is Pecola going to take of the white culture that surrounds her when it is measured against her own racial self-loathing?

So far, as I am sure you have noticed, I have made only passing reference to the International Baccalaureate. That is deliberate because today's theme is bigger, much bigger, than any particular programme of education. However, in the few minutes that remain I am going to use one of the IB's programmes to illustrate some of the points I have been making. I have chosen the IB Middle Years Programme (MYP), designed for students who are in that critical period of adolescence from ages roughly 11 to 16. Again, this is not an appropriate moment to go into detail, but I want to highlight four key factors in that programme, which is now being taught in 500 schools in more than 60 different countries:

1. It requires study in eight areas of learning: the mother tongue, a foreign language, maths, science, humanities, technology, physical education and the arts. Global citizens need to develop well-honed academic skills – to use Thomas Friedman's description, they need business school minds coupled to social worker hearts.
2. However, each of these eight disciplines is not studied in isolation. They are brought together by five so-called 'areas of interaction': approaches to learning, community and service, *homo faber* (why and how we create and what are the circumstances), the environment, and health and social education. In other words the disciplinary learning is focused through the areas of interaction on issues that directly relate to the students' lives.
3. Each student is required to complete a personal project as the culmination of a sustained involvement with the areas of interaction and requiring (as Kurt Hahn would have put it): 'Victorious patience and tenacity of effort – carried through to a well defined end and designed to tap the hidden reserves of intellect and will.'
4. The overarching themes of cultural awareness and communication are present as a constant reminder in the teachers' guides to the programme.

The Middle Years Programme is essentially a framework within which different content, different emphases and different national traditions can be accommodated. The MYP that I have seen in Binghamton, taught of course in English, is different to the MYP I have seen in Beijing, taught in Chinese, but they are recognisably the same programme, based on the same values and using the same guidelines. It is prescriptive in one important sense: it requires students and teachers to look beyond the horizons of their own cultural experience. It does not, however, seek to replace or to undermine that experience, but to use it as a starting point in the quest that President Bush described so well in that sentence:

> I want you to know that I am interested in not only how you talk but how you live.

In conclusion I return to my lecture's title which poses the question: 'Education: for the nation or for the world?' I hope by now that I have persuaded you that the title needs two changes: first by replacing *or* with *and* second by removing the question mark. Let it become 'Education: for the nation and for the world'. We have no choice. Whether or not it is our individual human instinct to reach out to others, or to be fearful of others reaching out to us, the impact of globalization means that neither process can be stopped, still less reversed.

To remind you of Bronfenbrenner's definition, we are dealing with the 'concern of one generation for the next'. Our children and our grandchildren will always live in a globalized world and their education must equip them with appropriate knowledge, skills and values as best we can currently describe them.

Let me then finish with the words of Mahatma Gandhi:

> I do not want my house to be walled in on all sides and my windows to be stuffed. I want the cultures of all the lands to be blown about my house as freely as possible. But I refuse to be blown off my feet by any. I refuse to live in other people's houses as an interloper, a beggar or a slave... Mine is not a religion of the prison-house. It has room for the least among God's creation. But it is proof against insolence, pride of race, religion or colour.

Schools as Cultural Crossroads

International School of Geneva

7 January 2006

Introduction

You must forgive me if I seem to approach today's conference with just a small element of irresponsibility, but as recently as a week ago I was in charge of the International Baccalaureate (IB). Today I no longer am. Instead, I am in a rather pleasant state of limbo with the title of 'director general emeritus' whose only practical meaning can be that I am allowed to say what I want to say on any subject. And in four months' time I shall have retired and it will be too late to catch up with me!

So, if today's emphasis is one of questioning rather than telling, of probing rather than confirming, then I hope you will understand. And if any of the questioning and probing is aimed at the IB then I do it with a clear conscience because, without hesitation, I accept full responsibility for what has happened to that organization during the past six years.

My first probe is directed towards the conference title, *Schools as Cultural Crossroads*, which allows two rather different interpretations. The first, which is explained by Dr Tate in his foreword to the programme, places international schools (such as our host, the International School of Geneva, Ecolint,) at an important cultural meeting place. Just as the key geographical crossroads of Byzantium, Samarkand, and indeed Geneva itself, attracted merchants of diverse cultures to conduct business together, so international schools attract students, parents and teachers of diverse cultures to conduct education together.

But the second reason for being at a crossroads is to make a choice, either to keep going or to select a different direction. For me this is the more challenging interpretation, *first* because it embraces all schools, national and international, state and private, all of which should be asking how best to respond to the educational challenges of globalization and *second* because it requires those international schools that sit at privileged cross roads throughout the world to ask if they are really achieving all that they are claiming. As I have pointed out elsewhere[1] those claims are not trivial and include such ambitious targets as 'preparation of students for the reintegration into their own cultures or for integration into other cultures', 'finding themselves at home in all cultures and human situations' and 'going further and deeper, really to grasp another person's values'. Well... I just wonder.

The evidence for success in this area of endeavour is not encouraging, largely because so little exists. There is plenty of research evidence confirming the importance ascribed by international school students and their teachers to *encouraging* cultural awareness but there is little evidence to support its *achievement*, still less to indicate that one method rather than another is perhaps more effective. Instead, there is evidence of the isolation of international schools from their local communities; of the US and the UK dominating curricula and styles of learning; and of national cliques forming within the international communities of students. There is also anecdotal evidence of reversion to national, even nationalistic, stereotype during periods of international tension and I have quoted[2] the astonishing online exchange that took place between four Serbian graduates of Ecolint during the NATO bombing of Kosovo in 1999. There was little evidence there of being able to 'grasp another person's values'.

In some ways the IB itself can be part of the problem, rather than the solution. I have often thought that the IB's biggest challenge is not having a big enough challenge from any serious competitor, rival or alternative organization. There are therefore occasions when international education is conveniently defined in terms of IB programmes, IB assessment and IB teacher training. It's rather like calling all vacuum cleaners by the brand name 'Hoover'. International education is the IB; the IB is international education.

Well, I don't believe it. Thinking about culture goes beyond thinking about the IB and that explains what I am *not* going to talk about today. I am not going to take you through a blow-by-blow account of how the IB, in its Primary Years, Middle Years and Diploma Programmes, tries to develop a greater cultural awareness in its students. From a practical point of view, I am aware that many of you in today's audience could use your daily experience of our programmes to achieve that task far more lucidly than I could. Instead, I am going to indicate some of the broad directions that I think schools should be considering as, throughout the world, they begin to find themselves at different cultural crossroads and wondering what direction to select. You can then tell me to what extent IB programmes encourage them to make the right choice.

Cultural we and cultural they

All good sermons must have a text and mine is taken from the novel *Snow* by one of my favourite writers, the Turkish author, Orhan Pamuk.[3] Pamuk, who is widely tipped to become a future Nobel literature prizewinner, is currently standing trial in Turkey for 'insulting Turkishness'. The main character in *Snow* says:

> I myself was not immune to the power of that shimmering fiction that any citizen of an oppressive and aggressively nationalistic country will understand only too well – the magical unity conjured by the word 'we'.

I shall return to Pamuk in a moment. But let me illustrate that 'we-feeling' by inviting you to eavesdrop on a conversation that took place last August at the headquarters of the IB, just across the road.

In the main office three francophone colleagues are working, but today we have a visitor from the UK, our treasurer, Joe Clinch, who is revising a financial document. I am working next door but, since lunchtime, I have been regularly visiting the *BBC News* website. I do so again, walk into the main office and say to Joe: "We are 129 for four, Joe." "Oh, dear," he replies, "it's going to be a very close finish."

Those 20 words split the office straight down the middle between 'we' (Joe and I) who enjoyed a moment of shared belonging while 'they' (the others) experienced a moment of complete alienation. In similar fashion I have split my audience today between those who understand cricket and those who don't. It is a trivial example perhaps but one, as we shall see, that illustrates many of the significant features of cultural identity.

The whole purpose of a culture is to signify belonging, which, at the same time, confirms exclusion. When TS Eliot[4] famously described a shared culture as 'what makes life worth living' he had no regrets about excluding those who did not share it. We can be fairly sure that Eliot found life *more* worth living without those around him who did not share his culture.

In his introduction Dr Tate mentioned Matthew Arnold and for me, one of the great attractions of Arnold is that he did want to share his culture with others. In his most famous essay,[5] he wrote:

> (Culture) seeks to do away with classes; to make the best that has been thought and known in the world current everywhere; to make all men live in an atmosphere of sweetness and light, where they

may use ideas, as it uses them itself, freely – nourished, and not bound by them.

A culture confirms our identity, our belonging, which is arguably the most precious thing we possess and its influence is so powerful that I try to avoid the phrase 'cultural understanding' (believing this to be an impossible goal), preferring instead 'cultural awareness'.

Taught not caught

At this point I am going to label my signpost to read **cultural awareness is taught**. I doubt that anyone can ever step into the cultural shoes of another person but we can certainly develop our students' understanding of the importance of culture and of some of its consequences for human behaviour. This will not be achieved by merely 'rubbing shoulders' with people of different cultural backgrounds. On the contrary, the process requires the same careful planning that we would devote to learning about physics, or history or music.

This is the clear message that is contained in the remarkable UNESCO pamphlet of 1948[6] written by the former director of Ecolint, Marie Thérèse Maurette. I do not have time to describe it in detail but it remains one of the most radical contributions ever made to the subject of international education (which she called *Education pour la Paix*), so let me quickly list the main points upon which she insisted such an education would be constructed:

1. total respect for each student's nationality: there were to be no first and second class nationalities in her school;
2. an emphasis on the international rather than the national, particularly in geography and history, even to the extent of designing a new world atlas;
3. the acquisition of a second language with the goal of bilingualism;
4. regular meetings of the whole school to discuss current world affairs; and
5. team activities including a strong element of community service.

For my purpose today, the detail is unimportant and on some issues she was probably, in retrospect, wrong. The point I am making is that nearly 60 years ago, Mme Maurette was insisting that cultural awareness does not happen by chance, or by some natural process of osmosis, or even by sharing one's education with students of other nationalities. It has to be addressed through the school's formal curriculum, its extra curriculum and its hidden curriculum.

A cultural model

I am now going to add a second destination to my signpost and it reads **the software of the mind**. This reminds me of the description of culture proposed by Geert Hofstede[7] who has done more than anyone to help me understand the significance of culture in the multicultural workplace. Our culture programmes the way we perceive the world and determines how, indeed *if*, we are able to share our thoughts with others. It's as though I had carefully prepared a PowerPoint presentation for a colleague but he has not installed the right software in his computer and simply cannot open it. I am therefore forced to go back to the presentation and rework it into a receivable format, which, inevitably, will not be quite what I had intended. We have to reach a compromise.

Hofstede models culture like an onion, with symbols, heroes and rituals occupying successive layers as you move closer to the centre. I find this a helpful model because these are a culture's observable practices, which can be studied at different levels of sophistication depending upon the age of the student. At the simplest level they can be linked to the much-disparaged 5Fs: food, fashion, festivals, folklore and famous people, but let us imagine older students trying to make cultural sense of the following poem (and this, I promise, is my final reference to the game of cricket!)

> There's a breathless hush in the Close tonight –
> Ten to make and the match to win –
> A bumping pitch and a blinding light,
> An hour to play and the last man in.
> And it's not for the sake of the ribboned coat,
> Or the selfish hope of a season's fame,
> But his Captain's hand on his shoulder smote
> "Play up! Play up! And play the game!"
>
> The sand of the desert is sodden red, –
> Red with the wreck of a square that broke; –
> The Gatling's jammed and the Colonel dead,
> And the regiment blind with dust and smoke.
> The river of death has brimmed its banks,
> And England's far, and Honour a name,

> But the voice of schoolboy rallies the ranks,
> "Play up! Play up! And play the game!"
>
> This is the word that year by year
> While in her place the School is set
> Every one of her sons must hear,
> Ands none that hears it dare forget.
> This they all with a joyful mind
> Bear through life like a torch in flame,
> And falling fling to the host behind –
> "Play up, play up and play the game!"

I have quoted that poem[8] in its entirety because it illustrates so vividly the way in which an apparently neutral, innocent cultural pastime, played with a bat and ball, becomes embellished with a distinctive set of heroes and rituals, is reinforced by a particular system of education, and thus comes to symbolise a powerful set of values, familiar not only to the poet, but to those around him who belong to his culture. It will not surprise you to learn that the author, Henry Newbolt, was put in charge of British propaganda during the First World War!

So, at the heart of Hofstede's onion model lie the values of the culture, which he describes as 'broad tendencies to prefer certain states of affairs over others' and it is in following this signpost that our students begin to understand how those unfamiliar, and sometimes shocking, observable differences are manifestations of significantly different values, often of religious origin. A colleague, for example, was recently telling me of her distaste on learning that a man in a village in Southern Africa was taking another bride, aged 15, to replace those who were becoming too old for him. But he was just as shocked to learn that she lived completely on her own in Britain without any immediate family support, unlike his new bride who would be protected within a large family unit against poverty. This is just one example of culture shock to which you could add many others, from your own daily experience.

The IB seems to take a clear view about this: 'other people with their differences can also be right' – it is the final and most argued-over sentence of our mission statement. But what if this man, through his sexual behaviour, is encouraging the spread of HIV/AIDS in his community? Is he still right? And if he is not, is it not the responsibility of educators to persuade him that he is wrong and that his culture must adapt to change. 'This is what makes education a somewhat dangerous pursuit.'

Practical advice

Those last words are not mine. They belong to someone else who, despite his international eminence, has never forgotten the reality under which teachers actually operate, day by day, week by week and year by year: the American developmental psychologist, Jerome Bruner.

> Meaning making involves situating encounters with the world in their appropriate cultural contexts in order to know "what they are about." Although meanings are "in the mind" they have their origins and their significance in the culture in which they are created.[9]

Bruner suggests a number of practical consequences for teaching in a multicultural environment and I have selected five of them for my signpost. I hope that as I summarise them, you will reflect on your own experience and, where appropriate, put it into the context of the IB programmes:

- The meaning of something depends on the frame of reference in which it is perceived. I said I would return to the Turkish writer, Orhan Pamuk, and to his trial for 'insulting Turkishness' because this illustrates Bruner's point. According to the Turkish government, about 50,000 Armenians lost their lives in 1915 as war casualties. According to Pamuk (and many historians) more than one million Armenians were massacred by the Turks in an act of genocide. Pamuk's trial has been suspended while the Turkish Government considers its position because now a third perspective is emerging to influence the official view of the events of 1915: Turkey's desire for membership of the European Union.

- Bruner stresses the importance of 'thinking about thinking' and, in particular trying to distinguish between that which is innate and that which is culturally interpreted. We cannot, for example, imagine time running backwards or space contracting but anthropologists will point to culturally different variations of time and space. We cannot imagine abandoning the notion of prior thought affecting current thought and so building the concept of responsibility. But the interpretation of 'responsibility' in different cultures differs widely. I keep reminding myself that the South African Commission for Reconciliation and Truth, chaired by Archbishop Desmond Tutu, devised no fewer than three acceptable definitions of truth.

- Bruner's third point concerns what he believes to be the

exceptional human ability to understand the mind of others, using language certainly, but also gesture and other means. He calls this 'intersubjectivity' and writes:

> Our Western pedagogical tradition hardly does justice to the importance of intersubjectivity in transmitting culture. Indeed, it often clings to a preference for a degree of explicitness that seems to ignore it. So teaching is fitted into a mould in which a single, presumably omniscient teacher explicitly tells or shows presumably unknowing learners something they presumably know nothing about… One of the most radical proposals to have emerged from the cultural-psychological approach to education is that the classroom be reconceived as … a subcommunity of mutual learners, with the teacher orchestrating proceedings.

- The fourth point that I have chosen highlights the importance of what Bruner calls 'œuvres' – tangible expressions of learning that 'give pride, identity and a sense of community to those who participate'. I would take a small bet that most of your memories of school, including those of some of your most productive relationships with other students and teachers, are associated with your contribution to such œuvres – the drama production, the science exhibition, the presentation of the school trip video to parents, the Yearbook, the Students' United Nations and so on.

- Finally, Bruner suggests there are two main ways in which human beings manage their knowledge of the world: logical-scientific thinking and narrative thinking. 'No culture is without both of them, though different cultures privilege them differently.' Not surprisingly, he believes that the encouragement of narrative thinking – song, drama, fiction, theatre, whatever – is greatly undervalued, treated as a decoration rather than a necessity. At which point I think I can take some pride in the importance attached to world literature in the IB Diploma Programme, but once again experience that stab of guilt that we do not insist that every diploma student should study a subject from Group 6, the arts.

Inclusion brings exclusion

I am now going to paint my fourth and final direction onto that signpost at our cultural crossroads, but first let's just remind ourselves what is up there already.

The **first** direction said that cultural awareness is taught; it does not happen by chance.

The **second** proposed a simple model of culture; there are others but Hofstede's is one that I personally find helpful as a basis for actually studying and comparing cultures.

The **third**, filling in some of the detail of that model, was the practical classroom advice from Jerome Bruner. (By the way: can it be entirely coincidental that Bruner spent the Second World War working on propaganda with the US Army's Intelligence Corps?)

Now, my **fourth** direction takes me back to an earlier point, when I spoke of the way our culture confirms our identity, through our sense of belonging. To be left out in the cold, to be excluded, by the game of cricket does not matter very much, but to belong to an oppressed minority culture, to be confined to an environment where no one understands my language, or to see the entire world being slowly infiltrated by the culture of the single remaining superpower: that can matter very much indeed because each threatens my capacity to be who I want to be, to belong where I want to belong. They threaten my very identity.

No one has written more convincingly on the subject of identity than the Lebanese/French novelist Amin Maalouf. He writes of Lebanon, where he was born:

> ...that is a country where you are constantly having to question yourself about your affiliations, your origins, your relationships with others, and your possible place in the sun or in the shade.[10]

And he questions what he believes is the fundamentally dangerous idea that identity means a single affiliation:

> ...the idea I'm challenging – the notion that reduces identity to one single affiliation – encourages people to adopt an attitude that is partial, sectarian, intolerant, domineering, sometimes suicidal, and frequently even changes them into killers or supporters of killers.

On the other hand, he writes:

> When one sees one's own identity as made up of a number of allegiances, some linked to an ethnic past and others not, some linked to a religious tradition and others not; when one observes in oneself, in one's origins and in the course one's life has taken, a number of different confluences and contributions, of different

mixtures and influences, some of them quite subtle or even incompatible with one another; then one enters into a different relationship both with other people and with one's own "tribe". It's no longer just a question of "them" and "us"…

Some of you will have noticed that I have deliberately avoided today the concept of the so-called Third Culture Kid (TCK), who has neither the culture of his passport nor the culture of where he happens to be living at the moment – a well known phenomenon of most international schools. Should we pity the TCK for lacking a single, dominant thread of cultural affiliation or should we instead perceive the TCK's multiple affiliations as a positive model for the future? I will leave someone else to develop that hypothesis, but Maalouf's words do seem to give the idea some credence:

> As long as an individual's place in society goes on depending on his belonging to some community or other we are perpetuating a perverse state of affairs that can only deepen divisions.

So my final direction reads **threads of affiliation** and encourages us to do everything possible to give our students starting points from which multiple threads of cultural affiliation can be built on, and developed, throughout their lives.

And the IB…?

I have already made a number of specific references to the IB's contribution to my four signpost directions. Now, in conclusion, let me make some very brief, but more general, observations about the IB in the context of today's conference:

1. Our values, as expressed in our Act of Foundation, our mission statement and in our newly developed learner profile are entirely consistent with the encouragement of cultural awareness. It is a clearly expressed priority for the organization.

2. The emphasis on critical thinking, inquiry, constructivism and teamwork, which are all important features of the three IB programmes, helps to develop appropriate intellectual tools for studying different cultures.

3. Each one of the subject disciplines in the Middle Years and the Diploma Programmes is open to interpretation and development in ways that illustrate different cultural dimensions and contributions.

4. The IB's emphasis on languages makes an important contribution to learning about different cultures. Maalouf, incidentally, proposes three languages for every student: the mother tongue (for identity), English (for communication) and a third language (for diversity).

5. Finally, there are the particularly distinctive elements of the IB's programmes such as the Exhibition, the Areas of Interaction, Theory of Knowledge and CAS which offer very special opportunities for learning more about different cultures and about their interactions in a global society.

I think all this helps to point our students in the right direction as they move away from the crossroads. And the destination? Well, I would settle for the modest ambition of my predecessor, Roger Peel, who wrote:

> It is not expected that students adopt alien points of view, merely that they are exposed to them and encouraged to respond intelligently. The end result, we hope, is a more compassionate population, a welcome manifestation of national diversity within an international framework of tolerant respect.[11]

And I am going to end by quoting Alec Peterson, whom many would call the father of the IB, who replied as follows when asked what were the goals of the IB:

> ...to develop to their fullest potential the powers of each individual to understand, to modify and to enjoy his or her environment, both inner and outer, in its physical, social, moral, aesthetic and spiritual dimensions.[12]

The word 'culture' does not appear at all, but most of what I have just been talking about most certainly does.

References

1. Walker, G. (2000): One-Way Streets of our Culture, in *International Schools Journal*, Vol XIX, No 2, pp11-19.
2. Walker, G. (2004): *To Educate the Nations 2*. Suffolk, Peridot Press. p62.
3. Pamuk, O. (2004): *Snow*. London, Faber.
4. Eliot, T S. (1948): *Notes Towards a Definition of Culture*. London, Faber & Faber.
5. Arnold, M. (1883): *Culture and Anarchy*. London, Macmillan & Co.
6. Maurette, M. T. (1948): *Techniques d'éducation pour la paix: Existent-elles?* Paris, UNESCO. SS/TAIU/9.

7. Hofstede, G. H. (2004): *Cultures and Organizations*. New York, McGraw-Hill.
8. Newbolt, H. (1897): *Vitaï Lampada*.
9. Bruner, J. S. (1996): *The Culture of Education*. MA, Harvard University Press.
10. Maalouf, A. (2000): *In the Name of Identity: violence and need to belong*. New York, Arcade Publishing.
11. *Education for Life*. UNESCO, International Baccalaureate Organisation, 2005.
12. Peterson, A. D. C. (2003): *Schools Across Frontiers. The Story of the International Baccalaureate and the United World Colleges*. IL, Open Court. Second edition.

Global Warming

25th Opening Ceremony of United World College of the Adriatic

Teatro Verdi, Trieste

20 October 2007

Distinguished Guests, Ladies and Gentlemen and especially Young Ladies and Gentlemen – today's students:

Thank you for inviting me to this very special occasion; it is both a pleasure and an honour to be speaking to you. And let me start by congratulating you on your 25th birthday – your silver jubilee. It is a very important achievement but have you ever wondered why 25 is so special?

Well, first it's a nice rounded number: a quarter of a century; a numerical square that is (as Pythagoras realized) the sum of two other squares. It is also the smallest Friedman number, but you'll have to ask a math teacher to explain that.

But, more important, 25 has a special human significance. It is sometimes used to signal the official end of youth so we can confidently say the United World College of the Adriatic has reached adulthood – no excuses for adolescent behaviour! And 25 years roughly spans the gap between the generations: the distance between grandparent and parent, parent and child, child and grandchild. It is also a practical time span – I can still remember what I was doing 25 years ago. Alas, I can also remember what I was doing 25 years before that!

So for someone of my age, anniversaries are all about looking back, usually with some nostalgia. For today's students that is clearly impossible: 25 years makes sense in only one direction and that direction is forward, towards the future. So for the next few minutes I am going to talk about what the next 25 years might look like and how you can best prepare for them. We are about to engage in a risky business: future planning, scenario designing, crystal ball gazing. There was a time when you could simply take a ruler and extend the experience of the past 25 years straight into the next 25. Those days have long since gone.

Back in 1982, for example, who could possibly have foreseen the global impact of HIV/AIDS, the dismantling of the Berlin Wall, the civil war across nearby borders in former Yugoslavia, the political transformation of South

Africa, the terrible events of 9/11, the impact of computer technology and of digital communication? Who dared to imagine that Italy would win the 2006 World Cup?

Well, the fact is that most of those events could have been, and indeed were, predicted by people whose job it is to study long-term trends and historical precedents and to project them into the future. Apartheid in South Africa was an unsustainable aberration; Yugoslavia without Tito had become ungovernable; communism in Eastern Europe was in retreat as early as 1970. Even I had seen enough during several visits to Baghdad to predict with some accuracy today's appalling mess in Iraq. The 21st century world may be complex but it is nonetheless possible to make out important future developments for those who are prepared to listen and take notice.

What issues then will dominate the next 25 years? What will we (*you* more likely; not me!) be talking about in 2032? The onward march of militant Islam? China assuming pole position as the world's dominant economic power? The slow crumbling of free market economics under the burden of unsustainable social inequality? All these will be on the agenda, but I believe they will be overshadowed by one single, overwhelming issue: the impact of global warming. This, I believe, will be the major challenge during the most productive period of our students' lives.

After many years of argument four facts are now, I believe, universally accepted:

1. The earth's atmosphere is warming up.
2. This is caused by an increasing concentration of so-called 'greenhouse gases', notably carbon dioxide.
3. This increase is caused by human activity.
4. Global warming will produce a significant change in the earth's climate.

In case anyone still thinks this is interesting but unimportant and, given time, it will all blow away, let me quote from a recent report of the much respected International Institute for Strategic Studies, based in London, which warns that climate change could inflict catastrophic damage 'on the level of a nuclear war'. Since it was the threat of nuclear war that influenced the founding of the first United World College, Atlantic College, in 1962, I make no apology for speaking about a challenge of similar proportions today.

Challenges from a New World

I am going to suggest that the challenge of global warming raises three questions that we need to engage with:

1. What is science doing about it?
2. How can governments manage it?
3. Who is going to protect the most vulnerable?

Let us look very briefly at each in turn.

* * * * *

There is only one group of people who might just be able to slow the effects of global warming to manageable proportions and those are scientists. You could, of course, argue that science and technology got us into this mess in the first place; what is certain is that only science and technology will be able to get us out of it. So thank heavens the IB insists that every diploma student shall study science.

- Why not trap all the carbon dioxide in a process known as 'sequestration', either chemically or biologically? For example, marine biologists are fertilizing the ocean to stimulate the growth of plankton which in turn absorbs the carbon dioxide.
- Why not turn the gas into diamonds? I reckon that one litre of carbon dioxide will produce about two carats of diamond, but is it possible? How many of you know how to calculate if it is feasible or not? It's actually quite simple!
- What about nuclear fission, which currently supplies about 16% of the world's electricity? What is the state of research into nuclear fusion that avoids the dangerous long-term problems of radioactive waste disposal?
- How realistic are wind and tidal power?
- What is going on in the development of biofuels that offer a realistic alternative to hydrocarbons?

I hope there are some of you here today who see these questions as your questions. I hope many of you will want to make a substantial contribution to science and technology.

* * * * *

Whatever the scientists come up with, it will be the politicians that make the final decisions. And here we have a problem because the world's politics are not best organized to respond to global issues. We have heard a lot about the United States' refusal to sign up to the Kyoto Protocol but we hear less about those countries (Australia for example) that have signed the protocol but so far have refused to implement it. I would suggest that every country in the world is still putting national needs above global priorities. And the problem is more fundamental than that. Is a market economy ever going to support measures to deal with global warming; is a democracy the best form of political organization to address climate change? These are issues that need debating within the Theory of Knowledge and International Affairs courses.

I wonder how many of you have heard of the IPCC?[1] Well, it stands for the Intergovernmental Panel on Climate Change and it has become the most respected body in this field, an organization that really does seem to achieve consensus amongst different nations. Fortunately it is a committee of the United Nations. I say 'fortunately' because anything that brings credit to the UN should be welcomed because the United Nations is arguably the only organization that has the capability of coordinating a global response to climate change. The phrase 'think globally; act locally' has never been more appropriate and the UN will surely be the only political grouping to manage our global thinking.

I therefore hope that some of you here today will decide to work for the United Nations or for one of its international offspring like the World Health Organization, the International Labour Organization, the International Organization for Migration, the United Nations High Commission for Refugees and so on. They need the world's best minds so why not yours?

* * * * *

Finally, let us compare two consequences of global warming. The Adriatic is predicted to rise about 25cm during the 21st century with serious implications for the city of Venice. In a very different part of the world, about one fifth of the landmass of Bangladesh could disappear with the displacement of 20 million people and the reduction of the rice crop by a third. I need hardly tell you which problem – Venice or Bangladesh – is likely to attract the attention of the world's rich nations. More than 40 years ago an international charter was signed to guarantee the conservation and restoration of Venice. I am not aware of any international charter (except, perhaps, the Charter of the United Nations) that guarantees the conservation and restoration of Bangladesh.

The IB's mission statement urges students to be compassionate. Compassion does not mean feeling sorry for someone else's situation; it means doing something about it. Let us take the example of the Indian scholar, Amartya Sen, who was educated at one the world's earliest international schools in Bengal and has devoted his life to understanding the economics of poverty, for which he was awarded the Nobel Prize in 1998. Or take Muhammad Yunus and the Bangladeshi Grameen Bank, which offers small scale credit to fight poverty and was awarded the Nobel Peace Prize in 2006. Or the American project G1G1 (Give one Get one), which, by the end of November, will be selling two laptop computers loaded with educational software for US$399 – one for the purchaser and the other for a child in a developing country.

These are just three out of hundreds of examples of what is possible when the best brains are motivated by compassion. Have you considered using your brains and your very privileged education to become a social entrepreneur, someone who combines a 'business school brain with a social worker's heart' (Thomas Friedman's phrase)? Let me remind you that the mission statement of the United World Colleges does not just commit UWC students to the 'ideals of peace and justice, understanding and cooperation'. It commits them to the *implementation* of the ideals of peace and justice, understanding and cooperation; in other words, to doing something about it.

Let me summarise: I have suggested this morning that the consequences of global warming and climate change will dominate the 21st century. The IPCC, which I mentioned earlier, has already concluded that it is too late to turn the clock back; the effects are already with us so the challenge now is to limit the damage and to learn to live with the consequences. I believe living peacefully with the consequences is more likely to happen if the very brightest of today's students become scientists, or help to strengthen international organizations or become social entrepreneurs.

I have already used the phrase 'think globally and act locally' and to conclude I am going to put that into action. My wife and I flew to Trieste from London earlier in the week and tomorrow we shall fly back. I have checked the cost of offsetting the carbon emissions for which we are responsible and it is 20 euros. Here it is – and I hope it will be used to buy a small tree which will serve as a reminder of our very happy visit and your very happy birthday!

Challenges from a New World

Reference

1. Several weeks after writing this address the IPCC was awarded the Nobel Prize for Peace for 2007, shared with former US Vice-President, Al Gore.

The Sky's the Limit

International Baccalaureate Academic Staff Seminar, Cardiff
31 March 2008

Let me start with the IB's significant achievements in the 20th century:
- an internationally respected pre-university diploma;
- three values-based programmes of K-12 international education;
- a style of learning short-handed as 'critical thinking';
- a network of IB World Schools in more than 120 countries; and
- high quality professional development.

The IB was a child of its times. It provided unity within academic plurality; it responded to a growing mood of international awareness; it offered a practical means – school education – of bringing about a tiny thaw in relations between nations frozen by the Cold War; it promulgated a style of learning that was consistent with the steady spread of democracy. The pioneering spirit of the 20th century IB was accurately captured in the title of its semi-official history – *Schools across Frontiers*.[1]

Times have changed and in the 21st century frontiers no longer seem to matter very much. Globalization has eroded the independence of nation states and mass migration has brought cultural diversity to our doorsteps. We no longer need a passport to experience the famous 'international 5Fs' because four of them – food, fashion, festivals and famous people – can be found in infinite variety under the fifth – a national flag. A contemporary account of the IB might be more accurately entitled *Schools across Diverse Cultures*.

I believe that the IB programmes, taken as a continuum, can respond with confidence to the three most important challenges of 21st century globalization: difference, complexity and inequality:
- The IB's emphasis on cultural awareness prepares students for a world where diversity has become a feature of everyday life. Increasingly, we are living next to, working alongside, sharing our leisure with, choosing our partner from, people with different cultural backgrounds. Understanding and learning to respect and accommodate their priorities must form an essential part of any future education.

- The IB's critical thinking skills provide intellectual tools well suited to a robust democratic society. At the same time let us acknowledge that the IB has never been truly 'international'; it is founded upon the humanist values that have their roots in the Western Enlightenment.

- The IB's community service encourages students to think and act on behalf of those less fortunate than themselves. Globalization has polarized the haves from the have-nots and society will need to mobilize the very best brains if we are to redress the resulting dangerous instability. Understanding the origins of empathy, compassion and sacrifice will be a future priority of any education system in the developed world.[2]

So, is all well for the IB in the 21st century? Superficially yes, perhaps it is, but under the surface I can begin to detect more profound currents of change. This child of the 20th century has been nurtured to its maturity during four decades of steady growth, not just in the world's major economies, but in practically every sphere of human activity. The highest mountain has been climbed and the deepest ocean plumbed; every area of the planet's surface has been Googled into a readily accessible internet experience. We understand the molecular composition of most forms of life and stand on the brink, wondering whether to create some of them ourselves. Our access to all kinds of information seems to have reached the limit of our capacity to make sense of it.

But rather suddenly, perhaps during the past decade, we seem to have reached a tipping point. All the dreams that were encouraged by expansion have begun to turn into the fears we associate with contraction. Globalization is shrinking the world in terms of travel, communication and independent freedom of action. Is it also beginning to shrink the scope of our creative thinking? What physical challenges remain to stretch our imagination? What new social movements will fire our sense of justice? Will the 20th century phrase 'the sky's the limit' begin to acquire an exactly opposite and sinister meaning in the 21st century as the effects of global warming, and our responses to them, impose more and more everyday restrictions on our lives?

I am going to highlight three ways in which I believe the focus of our thinking is likely to change in the decades ahead. In doing so I shall introduce three 'polarities', contrasting positions, that the IB will have to recognize and address in its programmes.

Climate change

I have argued elsewhere[3] that the impact of global warming on the earth's climate will dwarf every other future concern. Quite simply, the capacity of the planet to sustain human life at its present level, never mind at its projected level, is at serious and increasing risk. On the one hand we shall look to scientists, technologists and engineers to devise realistic ways of reversing the increasing concentration of atmospheric greenhouse gases and – perhaps under the ground, under the seas or in outer space – to compensate for the inevitable reduction in habitable and arable land. Their ingenuity may well determine the future of humankind, but this will take time and they must be allowed to make their inevitable mistakes along the way.

On the other hand, we shall have to grow accustomed to increasing government control with more rules and regulations for this, that and the other in a desperate attempt to slow down the destruction of the planet's atmosphere. 'Thou shalt not drive that car, fly in that aircraft, grow that crop, buy that vegetable, burn that refuse, holiday on that island…'

So here we have our first polarity: more central control over our daily lives versus the intellectual freedom needed to stimulate imaginative solutions to a profoundly threatening problem. Clearly science and related subjects like technology and engineering will find themselves in the spotlight, but to understand where we are, how we got there and what is acceptable as a way forward, literature, the creative arts and the humanities will be no less important.

Does it matter that our great-grandchildren may never walk on a glacier or see a snow-capped mountain? Is the loss any different from the dodo or the Hanging Gardens of Babylon? What will the traditional disciplines have to offer in an apparently diminishing world?

Universal values

I have already made reference to the essentially liberal, western style of thinking that underlies the IB's three programmes: they promote active inquiry, seeking objective evidence and questioning authority, even daring to say 'no' to God. Such thinking has long been regarded as the very foundation of the concept of democracy and more controversially of its closely associated free market economies. It would seem that the IB had backed a clear winner as first the unraveling of 19th century empires and then the dramatic collapse of the Soviet Union spread 'democracy' around the globe.

More recently, however, there are signs of a change in mood. The transplanting of the Athenian concept (or more accurately the Westminster concept) of 'democracy' to Iraq, Afghanistan and Palestine has stretched international credibility. The unchallenged superiority of free markets has been tarnished by destructive financial scandals and a breathtakingly irresponsible attitude to servicing debt. Western assumptions about 'human rights' are openly flouted in countries across the globe – China, Iran, Russia and Venezuela for example – without any apparent impact on their political influence and economic growth.

As different cultural traditions begin to overlap throughout the world, important values are called into question. Most recently in the United Kingdom, for example, media attention has been focused on arranged marriages and so-called 'honour killings'. The head of the established church, the Archbishop of Canterbury, caused a storm of criticism by suggesting that some aspects of Sharia law might usefully run alongside British law. The President of Uganda has upset the United Nations by refusing to hand over potential war criminals, arguing that they should be tried locally by a court that emphasizes reconciliation and compensation, rather than by the International Criminal Court in The Hague, which is predominantly concerned with punishment.

Here, then, is my second polarity; perhaps less of a polarity than a slow infiltration. The values of the 18th century Enlightenment are often described as universal values, a term that is explained and justified by reference to the United Nation's Declaration of Human Rights. But the western origins of the Universal Declaration are clear to see and hardly surprising when one lists those countries that held power and exerted influence when it was published in 1948.

A 21st century revision of the document might produce some interesting debate. Article 16 (2), for example, states: 'Marriage shall be entered into only with the free and full consent of the intending spouses.' And Article 19 states: 'Everyone has the right to freedom of opinion and expression.' Just how does that most famous aphorism of the Enlightenment (attributed to Voltaire) 'I detest what you say but will defend to the death your right to say it' square with the deliberately provocative publication in Denmark of cartoons known to be deeply offensive to Moslems? Shall I defend to the death your right to say anything?

The inner and outer self

It is a sign of changing times when one of the UK's most prestigious independent schools (Wellington College, an IB World School), backed by one of the UK's most prestigious universities (Cambridge), introduces a compulsory course for 14 and 15 year olds on wellbeing – referred to informally as a course on 'happiness'. It includes a study of the relationship between mind and body, the conscious and subconscious and the past, present, future and fantasy lives.

My third polarity contrasts the inner with the outer being, bringing us back to a familiar IB theme. Alec Peterson described the aims of the IB Diploma Programme as:

> ...to develop to their fullest potential the powers of each individual to understand, to modify and to enjoy his or her environment, both inner and outer, in its physical, social, moral, aesthetic and spiritual aspects.

Peterson was describing what, today, we might call a holistic education.

There is nothing new here; my favourite book on education, *What is and what might be*,[4] is divided into two halves entitled 'Path of Mechanical Obedience' and 'Path of Self-Realisation', an unashamed polemic on the neglect of the education of the soul. Kurt Hahn, a figure closely linked to the origins of the IB and sometimes unfairly associated with cold showers, rough seas and the motto *mens sana in corpore sano* (which he never used), promoted a balance between the inner and the outer self:

> I regard it as the foremost task of education to ensure the survival of these qualities: an enterprising curiosity, an undefeatable spirit, tenacity in pursuit, readiness for sensible self denial and above all compassion...

And in 1940, in a lecture in Liverpool Cathedral, he included, rather controversially, amongst his three essential virtues the love of 'aloneness', not a million miles away from Wellington College's 'stillness'.

Education has focused on the outer rather than the inner environment during the 20th century. The distinctive IB diploma hexagon, for example, identifies six essentially different disciplines through which we try to make sense of the world around us rather than the world within us: literature, language, the individual and societies, the empirical sciences, mathematics and the arts. During a period when the economic, rather than the social or personal, benefits of education have been emphasized, it has required an unusually enlightened and determined teacher to identify the 'inner' components of each of these disciplines.

But again times are changing and the growing influence on the training departments of many commercial organizations of the concept of 'emotional intelligence' is just one example. The psychological change from expansion to contraction, that I discussed earlier, will surely develop a deeper sense of internal reflection and it is not wholly fanciful to imagine a new IB hexagon representing the holistic elements of the academic, spiritual, emotional, ethical, physical and psychological.

Summary

In looking ahead to the environment in which the IB will operate in the next, let us say, 25 years, I have identified three different 'polarities':

- between increasing regulation caused by fear of climate change versus the intellectual freedom required to stimulate and implement ways of mitigating its effects.
- between the so-called 'universal values' promulgated by the western nations versus alternative values of different cultures that are assuming a greater world influence.
- between the importance afforded to our understanding of the external versus the internal environments of humankind.

How the IB positions itself relative to each of these polarities must be an issue for further debate.

References:

1. Peterson, A. (2003): *Schools across Frontiers*. Open Court, Chicago.
2. I developed these three consequences of globalization in a lecture given on 16 August 2007 at Renaissance College in Hong Kong. See page 22
3. This was contained in a lecture given at the 25th anniversary opening ceremony of the United World College of the Adriatic in Trieste on 20 October 2007. See page 65
4. Holmes, E (1911): *What is and what might be*. Constable & Co, London.

Teaching for Quality Education: the Example of Mr Chips

Conference of British Schools in the Middle East, Muscat
31 January 2007

I have to start with a confession because I have done something I have never done before. A week ago, I knew exactly how I was going to run this session and had even discussed my requirements for flip-charts, hand microphones and so on. Then, quite unexpectedly, I changed my mind. Let me explain…

I was going to present an interactive session entitled (as you well know) 'Teaching for Quality Education', though I must admit that I was going to ask permission to change the title into 'Teaching for Quality *Learning*'. I am sure you would not have objected; after all what's education for if it is not for learning?

I was going to start off by asking you to help me define some key features of quality learning, confident that between us we would arrive at something like the following list:

- learning that can be used in unfamiliar situations;
- learning that can be confidently built upon in the future; and
- learning that is concerned with significant issues;

though I think we might have argued about what makes a 'significant issue'!

I was then going to ask you to reflect on a piece of learning in your own life – as a pupil, student or an adult learner – that had been especially effective and to identify the key reasons for that success. Ideally (but there would not have been enough time) I would have asked you to do the same with a particularly *unsuccessful* piece of learning because if you are drawing conclusions from real life it usually helps to study both good and bad examples.

I was fairly sure that your feedback could be grouped (hence the flip charts) into four main categories:

- something about the teacher;
- about the student;

- about the structure of the lesson; and
- about the available resources.

Anyway, whatever your feedback, I think I could have persuaded you (this is called 'guided discovery'!) that the interaction of those four elements – teacher, student, structure and resources – lies at the heart of quality learning. In passing, please note that I was not necessarily locating this learning in a school building; nor was I necessarily assuming a conventional face-to-face relationship between teacher and student. Nothing that I have said eliminates the possibility of distance learning or online learning.

At this point I was going to examine in more detail a number of key features of each of those four elements. For example:

One: Resources

I had decided to talk about the pros and cons of the internet and link it to whiteboard (or SMART Board) technology in the classroom. I have observed a number of whiteboard lessons recently and I have been impressed by the robustness and flexibility of the technology and by the capacity of teachers to progress from a simple blackboard-like tool, to a means of achieving lively pupil interaction with sophisticated software and resources downloaded from the internet. Given the choice between this or banks of networked PCs or individually-owned laptops, I have no doubt which would get my vote.

Two: Structure

I was then going to share with you one of my favourite books on education, written by one of my favorite authors: Jerome Bruner's *The Process of Education*, first published in 1960 and still widely read. It has become one of the classic texts on teaching and learning. His chapter entitled 'The Importance of Structure' is what I would have focused on. Bruner writes about the importance of understanding the underlying deep structure of a subject, of the student's sense of discovery, of achieving the right balance between heurism (guided discovery) and assertion-and-proof, and of the inevitability (sometimes the desirability) of rote learning.

He states his famous dictum 'any subject can be taught to any child in some honest form' and writes about revisiting a topic in increasingly sophisticated fashion, constructing what he calls 'the spiral curriculum' (remember what we said earlier about being able to build on quality learning). He emphasizes the choice of the 'question of medium difficulty', just enough to lead the student on to the next stage of understanding. Finally, there is a fascinating chapter on intuitive and analytical thinking.

> The complementary nature of intuitive and analytic thinking should, we think, be recognized. Through intuitive thinking the individual may often arrive at solutions to problems which he would not achieve at all, or at best more slowly, through analytic thinking. Once achieved by intuitive methods, they should if possible be checked by analytical methods, while at the same time being respected as worthy hypotheses for such checking... Unfortunately, the formalism of school learning somehow devalued intuition.

Three: The Student

Discussing the role of the student was going to give me the opportunity to comment on the rather frustrating world of neuroscience. Frustrating, because there seems to be such rapid progress in our understanding of the brain, yet so little of it seems to trickle down into practical help for the teacher in the classroom. Instead, we have a number of myths that are based upon bogus science such as 'schools best suit girls' brains' or 'schools are designed for left-brained students' or 'young children's brains must have lots of sensory stimulation', all of which is proven nonsense.

Nonetheless, I have learned quite a lot from *The Learning Brain* by Blakemore and Frith (2005). For example:

- The brain is not just 'there' waiting to be used like a computer; it must be educated or trained by exposure to external stimuli. Use it or lose it. But it must be trained with good practice.
- There are some *sensitive periods* for developing particular parts of the brain; if you miss them compensation is possible but will probably be less satisfactory *eg* language (grammar, not vocabulary).
- Remedial action (often using an unfamiliar part of the brain) can be very powerful but it is much slower and needs more careful repetition.
- Much is known about disorders caused by brain malfunction: dyslexia, dyscalculia, autism, Asperger syndrome, ADHD, making possible their early diagnosis from brain scans.

- Adolescence brings another big learning opportunity (the frontal part of brain grows – controlling executive, decision-making functions) so age ten to 15 is as important as age nought to three.
- A huge amount is known about memory: episodic, semantic, procedural.
- The importance of sleep in the learning process is being better understood.

How can we use our brain power more effectively? We passionately believe that brain science will eventually give us answers to this important question. At the very least this belief can enhance our desire to learn and to teach.

Four: The Teacher

Finally, I had planned to talk about the fourth element of quality learning, the teacher. The teacher as communicator, as a model of competence and as a personal symbol of the process of education itself, a figure with whom students can identify and compare themselves (all those descriptions are taken from *The Process of Education*).

And at this point my preparation began to come off my carefully constructed rails. I made the fatal mistake of looking for a novel to illuminate the role of the teacher. I am convinced that we can learn as much from fiction as we can from fact; examples from literature can richly complement conventional academic study. Although novels are not necessarily carefully researched (many are, of course), they are written from a sense of passion and personal involvement that can convey uniquely powerful messages. So I turned to that classic story of school teaching, *Goodbye Mr Chips*. Written over 70 years ago, it has been filmed and televised many times and even turned into a West End musical. As a result it has become increasingly distorted, its true message gradually concealed under layers of accreted nostalgia and sentimentality.

I therefore went back to the original book, which has never been out of print since 1934, selling over two and a half million copies. I had not read it for years but how quickly one bonds with its hero, Mr Chipping, known simply as 'Chips'. Chips was never an outstanding scholar, so he has to be content with teaching classics at Brookfield, a second division independent school where he spends his entire career. As a young teacher, Chips has discipline problems and he has to struggle to overcome them.

Chips hates change though his brain tells him that the school must change with the times. Chips begins to use the same notes for his lessons year after year. We can all identify with Mr Chips!

So what is it about this unexceptional, rather dull schoolmaster that makes him so attractive? What is it about the book (which spans a 60-year period of Chips' life in less than 20,000 words – a remarkable tour de force) that has kept it alive all these years? Let me answer that question with a quotation. Chips has just been criticized by the new Head, Ralston, for his poor examination results.

> These examinations and certificates and so on – what did they matter? And all this efficiency and up-to-dateness – what did that matter either? Ralston was trying to run Brookfield like a factory – a factory for turning out a snob-culture based on money and machines... Vulgar ... ostentatious ... all the hectic rotten-ripeness of the age... No sense of proportion. And it was a sense of proportion, above all things, that Brookfield ought to teach.

'Sense of proportion' – that is the key to this book; a sense of balance. For example:

- Old aged is balanced against youth – Chips goes on to build an excellent relationship with Ralston's successor who is in his early thirties.
- Intense patriotism (but never jingoism) is balanced against internationalism, as in the famous passage when Chips (who has become acting-headmaster during the First World War) reads out the weekly list of old boys killed on the Western Front and, to the astonishment of the staff and boys, includes the name of the former German teacher, Max Staefel, who has died fighting for the enemy.
- The masculine ethos of the boys' school is balanced against the femininity of Chips' much younger wife, Katherine, who dies tragically in childbirth, a year after their marriage.
- The conservatism of Chips is balanced against the radicalism of his wife: 'her young idealism worked upon his maturity to produce an amalgam very gentle and wise.'
- Chips never takes himself too seriously; his dedication to his job is balanced against a keen sense of the ridiculous.

I want to suggest that this brief, old-fashioned and at times rather quaint book contains an essential lesson for the 21st century. Increasingly, we are expected to live our lives at the extremes. Physically, for example, every organized sport has been taken to its legal limits and, by those willing to risk detection, way beyond those limits. There is no room any more for the gifted amateur.

For our entertainment we are invited to watch the crude embarrassments and obscenities of 'Reality TV' and pretend, when forced to justify its excesses, that it helps us to understand better the social interactions of the real world around us. A real world, it would seem, that has no place for old-world courtesy, fair play and magnanimity.

In increasingly confrontational politics, polarization on every single issue sweeps everyone to the extremes of the debate and well-educated men and women are forced to defend the indefensible with arguments that insult their intelligence.

In the media, that much-prized but much-abused commodity, 'free expression', allows the British tabloid press to illustrate every story with a Muslim angle, with a photograph of a one-eyed, one-armed, bearded extremist (now conveniently in jail) in an uncontrolled rash of blatant Islamophobia.

Today, we must either be *for* something or *against* it. It is inconceivable to imagine an influential figure in any walk of British life – commerce, the church, politics, the armed forces – saying to an interviewer: "Well, I haven't actually decided yet; I'm still thinking about it. In fact I'm finding it rather hard to reach a conclusion." Even scientists who, by definition, haven't decided yet, are still thinking about it and find it hard to reach a conclusion, are expected to take up a position for or against whatever the latest controversial issue happens to be – global warming, stem cell research, ID cards, GM foods or (in Richard Dawkins' case) the very existence of God.

In March, we shall be commemorating the 200th anniversary of the abolition of slavery in the United Kingdom and this will provide a unique opportunity to set the record straight, and acknowledge the extent to which the United Kingdom's wealth was built upon the lives of at least ten million slaves who were shipped (about a million perishing on the voyage) from Africa to the Americas. This has never been a central part of UK history but, predictably, the extremists are already at work, with pressure groups demanding financial reparation. The reaction is equally predictable: once litigation is in the air, open debate is shut down.

Challenges from a New World

Last week I was in Athens, meeting with the governing board of the very distinguished Athens College. We were looking at the college's mission statement which contains the sentence, 'Our goal is to instill in our students, by teaching and by example, a strong sense of …' the Greek word was *metron,* which had been translated into English as 'measure'. But that does not describe adequately a word, indeed a philosophy, which occupied Aristotle's thinking. By *metron*, he meant appropriate, balanced, moderate, with a sense of proportion, achieving the golden mean between the extremes of defect and excess. So courage represents the balance between cowardice and rashness; modesty balances humility and pride; temperance balances self-indulgence and insensibility.

This, I think, is the message of *Goodbye Mr Chips*, the search for a sense of proportion in our lives. The confidence to combine the old-fashioned with the new-fangled; to derive as much satisfaction from a compromise as from an extreme position; to avoid the stereotypes of 'left' or 'right', 'liberal' or 'conservative'; to defend the right to say, at least for the moment, 'I have not made up my mind'.

A couple of months ago, I sat in on a history lesson in the new United World College in Mostar, in Bosnia-Herzegovina. Gazing out of the window at the surrounding ruins of buildings destroyed during the fighting of the 1990s, I couldn't help wondering whose history the students would be learning. The teacher was Finnish and very experienced. The subject was the birth of the industrial revolution in 18th century Britain. The resource was a selection of articles by distinguished historians, some arguing for the positive, and others for the negative, consequences of the industrial revolution. The students were a mixture of nationalities, most of them quite unfamiliar with this kind of inquiry-based learning. The debate was warming up, for and against as each student contributed a point of view. Kurt, sitting in the corner, had remained silent.

"What do you think, Kurt?" asked the teacher.

"I no longer know what to think," he replied.

"Don't worry, then, I'll come back later," said the teacher.

In that brief moment, in Kurt's honest admission, in his confidence to risk making it, and in the teacher's response, maintaining the thread of support, I knew I had witnessed teaching for quality learning.

I spoke earlier of three qualities of quality learning:

- learning that can be used in unfamiliar situations;
- learning that can be confidently built upon in the future; and
- learning that is concerned with significant issues.

And I now want to add a fourth:

- learning for *metron*, for maintaining a sense of proportion in our lives.

Doing No Harm

TASIS, Lugano

26 March 2009

I have recently been reading a biography of the famous crime writer, Agatha Christie, who died in 1976. In her old age she wrote a note to her second husband, the distinguished archaeologist, Max Mallowan, with the following thought:

> I think it would be very nice if at the end of our lives we could feel that we'd never done anyone any harm

An interesting comment from someone whose mind had, for so long, been engaged in devising more and more ingenious ways for one person to murder another!

But I don't think she had physical harm in mind. Nor do I believe she was trying to make a particularly deep philosophical observation along the lines, for example, of John Stuart Mills's famous statement about harm:

> The only purpose for which power can be rightfully exercised over any member of a civilized society, against his will, is to prevent harm to others…

More likely she was simply prompted by the Golden Rule of morality, usually summarized in the phrase: Do as you would be done by. Because I know what it is like to be harmed, I won't harm you.

If so, then another philosopher, Immanuel Kant, would insist that Agatha Christie was proposing a universal law, rather than just an agreement between husband and wife:

> Act only according to that maxim whereby you can at the same time will that it should become a universal law

And I don't think any of us would argue against Mrs Christie's maxim: 'Let us not do harm to others.' It's certainly worth exploring in more depth.

Now, I have to admit that all this amateur philosophizing would never have occurred to me, had I not been reading, at the same time, a report issued by the UK-based Children's Society entitled 'A Good Childhood'. It's a damning account of the harm being done to children in the United Kingdom by a combination of:

- increased family break-up;
- excessive consumer pressure;
- too much examination stress; and
- increasing inequality.

The result, concludes the report, is that one in six children suffering from serious emotional or behavioural problems, compared to one in ten some 15 years ago. The study lasted two years and involved more than 30,000 pieces of evidence, most of it coming from children themselves.

Those four contributing factors have been summed up in the single phrase of 'excessive individualism in society' or, as the media quickly headlined it, 'looking after number one'. The co-author of the report (Lord Layard) wrote:

> The change we need most is one that puts harmonious social relationships rather than the pursuit of private success at the centre of our value system.

Needless to say, the authors of the report see the school as the key to improving the situation.

So, what practical contribution can schools realistically make to ensure that children do not develop into harmful grown ups? How can you organize your students' learning so that they do not grow into selfish adults, always putting themselves first? At first I wrote, 'thinking only of themselves', but that would be ridiculous; no one can live a life without thinking of others around them: partners, children, parents, friends, neighbours. So let's stick with the phrase, 'putting themselves first'.

When I talk about these 'harmful adults' I do not imply physical harm though, heaven knows, far too many children, even in so-called developed countries, still suffer appalling physical abuse. Nor am I talking about financial harm, though we need to recognize the catastrophic effects that misguided, or unguided, individuals can have on innocent people, when they gamble with their money in the so-called 'free market'.

Let me instead define 'harm' in this context as: 'damage to a young person's self-esteem, confidence or security.' So, for example, the sadistic sports teacher who made me jump into a freezing outdoor swimming pool once a week undermined my confidence. The maths teacher's unpredictably violent temper regularly shattered my sense of security. On the other hand the history teacher who lent me his own books, after sixth form specialization prevented me from continuing with his subject, undoubtedly increased my self-esteem. All three examples, I believe, have influenced the way I think and behave.

I want to look briefly at **four** qualities that I believe schools should be developing in their students, as a wise investment in their adulthood:

1. Generosity.
2. A sense of sacrifice.
3. A balance between rights and responsibilities.
4. Cultural awareness.

I shall then go on to look rather briefly at one person's suggestions about how they might be developed. I hope I shall whet your appetite to find out more.

* * * * * *

Generosity is invariably perceived as a weak virtue. It suggests political naivity, lack of judgement, surrendering hard-won ground in negotiations, the very antithesis of 'getting ahead'.

Even generosity of thought seems in rare supply these days, as we continue to feed on the legacy of the swinging sixties, the decade that made everyone, from the senior politician to the revered religious figure, a legitimate target of vitriolic satire. Generous it was not, as it fed our all-too-eager sense of *schadenfreude*, our satisfaction at witnessing someone else's misfortune.

In reality, generosity is not a weak virtue at all. It involves shrewd judgement and calculated risk, usually based upon that most difficult-to-measure of all human virtues – trust. 'Give them an inch and they'll take a mile' – is a powerful English proverb and I cannot find a single saying recommending generosity to counterbalance it. But carefully considered and applied, generosity can transform a situation, begin to solve a puzzle or break a deadlock.

For example, last year saw the 60th anniversary of the Marshall Plan, America's massive contribution to the recovery and reconstruction of post-war Europe. The contrast with the punitive outcome of the 1919 Versailles Treaty could not have been greater, and although the cynic will say it was only intended as a barrier against the further spread of Soviet influence, we can surely still be inspired by Marshall's famous Harvard speech of 1947:

> Our policy is not directed against any country, but against hunger, poverty, desperation and chaos.

Perhaps the most important manifestation of the spirit of generosity in schools lies in the practice of forgiveness. Is there anyone present today who has not been grateful for being given a second chance, grateful to someone who turned a blind eye, grateful for the retribution that was never exacted? 'Be careful', we are so often warned, 'if you let them get away with it, the flood gates will open.' I think I can honestly say that during the whole of my career in education I never saw a single flood gate open.

* * * * * *

My second virtue, **sacrifice**, is certainly not perceived as a weak quality; indeed in the final analysis it is measured in lost lives. Living, as I do, in the English countryside, I am still amazed and moved by the war memorials that record each small village's sacrifice in two world wars, some families losing two, three, four young men in the First World War. So perhaps I need to choose another, less emotive word because I am asking no one to lay down their lives, but rather to accept the important principle of giving something up in order that someone else should benefit.

Let me take the French proverb: *il faut reculer pour mieux sauter* – you have to step back in order to jump higher – and reinterpret it. It becomes a particularly apt phrase if, by stepping back, you can prepare the way for *someone else* to jump higher. This is true sacrifice. So to encourage their children, parents must often step back and give up things they have always held dear (it may be as simple but as essential as a good night's sleep). Good teachers must know when to step back and allow their pupils to fly unassisted beyond their control.

At a different level, the most serious challenge facing humankind – I refer of course to global warming and its associated climate change – will be confronted only if those who have material goods in abundance are prepared to sacrifice some of them for the common good. Perhaps one beneficial outcome of the current global economic crisis will be the realization in the developed world that life can go on with far less; we can actually get by without two of everything.

> When the powerful in a state, face to face with the weak, are prepared to make financial sacrifices for them and to help them and to satisfy them, that is the time when you get, first, compassion and the end of isolation and the appearance of comradeship and mutual defence, and then civic agreement and then other benefits beyond the capacity of anyone to enumerate in full.

That statement by Democritus (c460-370 BC and better known for his atomic theory) has been described as 'the most remarkable single utterance of a political theorist of Ancient Greece'. Surely, if for no other reason than enlightened self-interest, the powerful are going to have to make sacrifices to help and satisfy the weak if serious social unrest is to be avoided in the months and years ahead.

* * * * * *

There was another important 60th anniversary last year – I suppose 1948 saw the first small shoots of optimism emerging after the Second World War. I am referring, of course, to the United Nations' Universal Declaration of Human Rights. I was disappointed by the lack of interest shown in this anniversary, which, it seemed to me, offered an important opportunity to take a fresh look at the Declaration with a view to improving it.

I believe it is a crucially important document; a serious attempt to bring together a set of universally-held values. It is of particular importance to those involved in international education because our celebration of diversity is necessarily balanced against our shared commitment to a common set of values. Without them we have to surrender the ground to the cultural relativists and in the end, accept that 'anything goes'.

And yet the Universal Declaration is showing its age and it reminds us that its origins lay in a smaller and more western-oriented United Nations (there were then only 58 members compared to 192 today). Moreover its language is to modern ears unacceptably masculine in tone. But its most serious weakness lies in the huge imbalance between rights and responsibilities, or 'duties' as they are called. Whereas there are 28 articles laying out our rights, only in the 29th do we read:

> Everyone has duties to the community in which alone the free and full development of his [sic] personality is possible.

My third proposal for reducing future harm is to teach young people that **rights** are always balanced by **responsibilities**. 'Balanced' is perhaps an inappropriate word; what I mean is rights are only made possible when people accept the responsibilities that are necessary to sustain them. For example, if (and I quote from Article 20) 'everyone has the right to freedom of peaceful assembly and association', then those who exercise this right have the responsibility to ensure that it does remain peaceful. But the responsibility extends much wider than that: we must all defend the right to freedom of peaceful assembly even though many of us will never want, or need, to take advantage of it.

I think it's a great pity that this anniversary went by without an attempt to address some of these defects. Perhaps the uneasy consensus that was reached 60 years ago on issues such as torture, choice of religion, and universal education is just too precarious to meddle with today. Perhaps the 1948 Declaration is as far as the world dares to go.

* * * * * *

Let's see how far we have come in the last few minutes. I started with Agatha Christie's rather unremarkable wish that one should try to spend one's life without doing harm to others. I linked this to a depressing study recently published in the UK, suggesting that serious harm is being done to children by adults who are consistently putting themselves and their own selfish desires first.

I went on to suggest three ways in which we might help to educate a new generation of adults to become less concerned with 'number one' and more concerned with those around them, particularly those for whom they have a responsibility. I have emphasized the relevance of two rather old-fashioned virtues – generosity and sacrifice – and suggested that human rights mean little unless balanced against human responsibilities.

Now to my fourth and final quality, which is **cultural awareness**. A generation ago one would have reserved such a quality for an international audience (such as I have today) but with the current pace of migration there is now a very high probability that you will live next to, work alongside, share your leisure time with, choose as your lifetime partner, someone from a very different cultural background. Cultural awareness and cultural understanding (which comes first, I wonder?) are therefore essential qualities in increasingly diverse societies. We must learn to live with difference and hopefully in this 200th anniversary year of the birth of Charles Darwin, we shall learn to understand the importance of difference and thus to celebrate human diversity.

Culture has been described as 'the software of the mind': it programmes our responses to various situations. To respond differently we have to make an effort to re-programme our instinct, which is not easy. I cannot fully trust my cultural hard-wiring because it immediately puts me at the centre of every situation and, at best, I 'tolerate' or 'accept' the different view of others around me. If I am more culturally sensitive I can try to make the effort to put someone else at the centre and ask: 'How does this situation appear to them?'

Let me remind you, therefore, of the final, rather controversial, sentence of the IB mission statement:

> These programmes encourage students across the world to become active, compassionate and lifelong learners who understand that other people, with their differences, can also be right.

Notice the phrase is 'can also be' right rather than necessarily 'are' right. We are back to cultural relativism and I want to quote Professor Howard Gardner at this point, in an extract taken from his book *Five Minds for the Future*. His five distinctive minds are disciplined, synthesizing, creating ethical and respectful and describing the last of these, he writes:

> ...I must try to understand other persons on their own terms, make an imaginative leap when necessary to convey my trust in them, and try so far as possible to make common cause with them and to be worthy of their trust. This stance does not mean that I ignore my own beliefs, nor that I necessarily accept or pardon all that I encounter... But I am obliged to make the effort, and not merely to assume that what I had once believed on the basis of scattered impressions is necessarily true. Such humility may, in turn, engender positive responses in others.

So, if we are to look beyond number one, if we want to avoid doing harm to others, I am suggesting we need to do everything possible to encourage:

- generosity;
- a sense of sacrifice;
- a balance of rights and responsibilities; and
- sensitivity towards people of other cultures.

* * * * * *

How do we encourage these qualities? At this point I am going to be very selective by introducing just one person who had much to say about the moral dimension of education. He is (quite wrongly) associated with cold showers, rough seas and the motto *mens sana in corpore sano* (which he never used). He promoted outdoor activity despite being an invalid himself for most of his adult life, caring passionately about others who were handicapped. He insisted that the shallow individualism of contemporary culture must be countered by a new spirit of service, remembering that service means time and talent, not ready cash.

I am talking about Kurt Hahn (see page 43).

Let me urge you to read more about Hahn (which you will find on an excellent website - www.KurtHahn.org) because I really only have time to mention his name and quote, for example, the Seven Laws of Salem. But these, I hope, will be enough to link him to the theme of my talk:

1. Give students the opportunity for self-discovery.
2. Make the students meet with triumph and defeat.
3. Give the students the opportunity of self-effacement (sacrifice) in the common cause.
4. Provide periods of silence (note his Liverpool Cathedral speech of 1940 emphasizing the love of enterprise, aloneness and skill).
5. Train the imagination.
6. Make games important but not predominant.
7. Free the sons of the wealthy and powerful from the enervating sense of privilege.

And his Six Declines of Modern Youth: the decline of:

- fitness,
- initiative and enterprise,
- memory and imagination,
- skill and care,
- self-discipline, and
- compassion.

But Hahn was not a moaner and he never lost his faith in the infinite capacities of young people. He was a man of action, directly concerned with the foundation of Atlantic College, the first of the United World Colleges. His influence on the IB was indirect but is clearly there to see today in the mission statement, student profile, balanced curriculum, the extended essay and of course CAS. In a sermon given in 1943, he observed:

> All of us are tempted by the sloth of habit, by the bitterness of failure and frustration, by the hardness born of success, by the pride of wealth, by the arrogance of knowledge, by the insolence of office; we are all continually tempted to disregard the rights of our fellow men in favour of our own interests... Our conscience is always struggling against what seem irresistible temptations, and against self-deception operating in the service of these temptations – of greed, of prestige, of malice, of comfort. Over these temptations conscience would triumph every time if it could call to its help a counterforce, an ally: an ally strong enough to draw off from the besetting temptations sufficient emotional power to make them resistible. Compassion is that ally...

I believe in the years ahead we are going to see more emphasis on moral values in education. This is nothing new. Thomas Arnold, the famous mid-19th century headmaster of Rugby School, was concerned only to educate 'Christian gentlemen'. John Dewey took a more practical line when he wrote about :'...the idea of responsibility, of obligation to do something, to produce something, in the world.' Howard Gardner (*Good Work*, 2001) sees no disjunction between productive work and sound moral values:

> People who do good work ... are concerned to act in a responsible fashion with respect toward their personal goals; their family friends, peers and colleagues; their mission or sense of calling; the institutions with which they are affiliated; and, lastly, the wider world – people they do not know, those who will come afterwards, and, in the grandest sense, to the planet or to God.

The development of a moral conscience has always been at the heart of formal education but we seem to have lost its pulse in recent years. We have been increasingly effective at encouraging young people to be to be smart, entrepreneurial, inventive, competitive and risk-taking but it is now evident that a large number of the brightest and the best, like Icarus, have flown much too close to the sun.

The time has come to redress the balance and the IB has a vital contribution to make because it:

... aims to develop inquiring, knowledgeable and caring young people who help to create a better and more peaceful world through intercultural understanding and respect.

To this end the IB works with schools, governments and international organizations to develop challenging programmes of international education and rigorous assessment.

These programmes encourage students across the world to become active, compassionate and lifelong learners who understand that other people, with their differences, can also be right.

And if that helps us all to do less harm to others then it will have been a very sound investment.

Think Globally; Act Locally

Graduation of the Campus des Nations, International School of Geneva
12 June 2009

When I was a boy, I lived in a house that was close to a very busy and dangerous major road, the scene of many accidents. Every morning I had to cross this road on my way to school. Of course when I was very young my mother would see me safely across but later on it became my responsibility and each morning my mother's parting words would be: "Mind how you cross the road." Every single morning – until she no longer knew she was saying it: "Mind how you cross the road."

She must have known that it was a complete waste of breath but I think it was a kind of fingers-crossed insurance policy, so that when I was finally hit by a speeding truck she could at least say: "Well, the very last thing I said to him was…"

I feel a bit like my mother as I address you today! Here are you, the graduating class of 2009, about to leave the predictable, reassuring security of school to cross a busy, uncertain road to begin the next stage of your lives. I have the task of giving you that final piece of advice. What can I say that is more helpful than: "Mind how you cross the road."

Well, I'm going to tell you a simple story. It's a story about a husband and wife called Mr and Mrs Cheshire who used to live in the village where I now live in England. It's a local, even a parochial, story but one that encompasses the globe. And it starts in a village called Cavendish.

* * * * * *

First a few words about the village itself which is in East Anglia, not far from Cambridge. It's very old and very pretty: a village green surrounded by thatched cottages and the village pub; a village pond still known by its Old English name as 'the waver'; the village shop, the village primary school, opened in 1863, with the original inscription still above the door which reads:

> Come ye children
> And hearken unto me
> I will teach you
> The Fear of the Lord

Challenges from a New World

Not bad for a school mission statement! And then, of course, there is the beautiful medieval church of St Mary.

As you might expect, not a lot happens in Cavendish. There was, of course, the terrible murder of a Government minister who was set upon by a gang of farm workers and hacked to death just outside the church where he was seeking sanctuary. But that was in 1381, during what became known as the Peasants' Revolt and not many people are left who remember it today!

* * * * * *

It came as a surprise, then, when the whole village was invited to the church a couple of weeks ago. It was clearly an important occasion: two bishops were there in their brightly coloured robes; the bells were ringing, the choir was singing and the church was packed to overflowing.

We were there to witness the unveiling of a plaque to commemorate the lives and the work of this remarkable couple, Mr and Mrs Cheshire, who had lived in the village and are now buried there, in the cemetery. By the way, their grave – most unusually in the middle of rural England – is surrounded by graves all marked with Polish names. I'll come back to that puzzle in a moment...

What can these two people possibly have done to deserve such a ceremony, such publicity, such a fuss? Well, I need to give you some clues:

- Mrs Cheshire was much better known by her maiden name, Sue Ryder. She was the founder of the Sue Ryder homes for sick and elderly people.
- Mr Cheshire was much better known as Group Captain Leonard Cheshire, VC, a hero of the British Royal Air Force in the Second World War. He was the founder of the Leonard Cheshire homes for the disabled.

* * * * * *

Let's look first at Sue Ryder. When the Second World War broke out in 1939 she was just sixteen and she trained as a nurse. Then a year later she joined the First Aid Nursing Yeomanry (FANY) and was posted to the Special Operations Executive (SOE) supporting agents parachuted into occupied Poland. Later she worked for SOE in North Africa and Italy while she was still a teenager. Towards the end of the war she was in Normandy immediately after the allied invasion. She kept a diary:

Challenges from a New World

> The strange, sad, shocked silence of these scenes by moonlight. Derelict landing craft. Seagulls crying. Torn clothing on barbed wire. Green mounds in minefields marking the place of the dead. POWs digging graves and lowering shrouds on stretchers. Notices that hang drunkenly from broken hinges in unexpected places: 'Out of Bounds', 'Water not drinkable'...

As the war ended, she found herself in the ruins of Poland helping to resettle refugees, and visiting prisoners who had taken to crime as the only option for survival in the post-war chaos of central Europe. Some of the refugees she brought back to Britain to live in her house in Cavendish. Many were victims of concentration camps and they never recovered sufficiently to return to Poland, which explains all those Polish graves in the Cavendish cemetery.

When Sue Ryder died in 2000, there were over 80 Ryder homes. Today the charity, Sue Ryder Care, provides four million hours of specialist care each year in 12 countries in Europe and Africa, for people suffering from cancer, multiple sclerosis, Huntington's disease, Parkinson's disease, motor neurone disease, stroke and brain injury.

Sue Ryder became Lady Ryder, a member of the British House of Lords, in 1978.

* * * * * *

In 1959, Sue Ryder married Group Captain Leonard Cheshire. He was the most decorated British pilot in the Second World War. His Victoria Cross was awarded not, as is customary, for one outstanding act of bravery but for a hundred: the number of missions he flew over Germany (the average number was 25).

At the invitation of the American government he witnessed the atomic explosion at Nagasaki, which deeply affected him, making him realize that humankind now possessed the means to destroy itself. In an interview with the British Prime Minister, he described a future in which nuclear weapons might be delivered by rockets travelling through space. Clement Attlee thought he had taken leave of his senses.

And indeed, by the end of the war, he was both mentally and physically shattered, unable to decide what to do with the rest of his life. He was just 28 years old.

One day a former Air Force colleague turned up at his house with terminal liver cancer and nowhere to live. Cheshire nursed him until he died and then decided to open his house to others needing similar love and care. It all grew from there.

Today there are 250 Cheshire homes in 55 different countries. In 1991 Leonard Cheshire became Lord Cheshire, like his wife a member of the British House of Lords. He died in 1992. The former Indian Prime Minister, Jawaharlal Nehru, had described him as 'the greatest man I have met since Gandhi'.

* * * * * *

These two people had lived in my village and the village community was now remembering their work. As I sat in the church listening to the remarkable story of their lives, it became apparent that Sue Ryder and Leonard Cheshire were born with two big advantages in life: loving parents and a very good education. At an unusually early age both had experienced the horrors of war, which had persuaded them to try to build a better world by giving their lives to the service of others: to the elderly, the terminally sick and the disabled.

That decision meant they would never become rich; that they would never live easy, comfortable lives; that they would never become celebrities. There is nothing glamorous or materially rewarding about looking after the elderly.

I think four lessons emerge from their example, that I want to pass on to those of you graduating today:

- Don't wait until you are old. Sue Ryder was just 21 when she was working with refugees in the appalling conditions of central Europe in 1945. Leonard Cheshire won his Victoria Cross at the age of 27. Old age brings no benefits that are worth waiting for: get on with it now. Seize every opportunity that comes your way.

- Don't wait until you are an expert. Neither Ryder nor Cheshire knew anything about caring for the disabled and elderly. No certificates, no diplomas and they made many mistakes but they learned quickly from them. Even so, they upset many people who wanted everything to 'go through the right channels'. And that brings me to the third lesson.

- Don't try to change the world by yourself. Make sure you acquire the skills to work with other people, and with other organizations, because however committed you are you will achieve very little on your own and you will quickly become disillusioned. Leonard Cheshire wrote: 'Leaders there have to be ... but in their hearts they know only too well that what has been attributed to them is in fact the achievement of the team to which they belong.'
- Finally: don't wait until the sun is shining. The world of 1945 was a scene of desolation brought about by human atrocities committed on an unparalleled scale. For Sue Ryder and Leonard Cheshire this was not the moment for negative recrimination or black depression; it was just the right moment for positive action. I hope you will remember the motto of the Republic of Geneva: *Post Tenebras Lux*: after the darkness comes light.

* * * * * *

Leonard Cheshire wrote:

> We need a vision, a dream. The vision should be the oneness, the essential and organic solidarity of the human family. The dream, that we each in our way make our personal contribution towards building unity and peace among us.

I hope that those of you graduating from the International School of Geneva today will agree with that vision ('the oneness, the essential and organic solidarity of the human family') and will ask: "What dream can I fulfill, what personal contribution can I make?"

The IB encourages its students to become 'active and compassionate' learners (I quote from its mission statement). I have chosen two examples today to show you how quite ordinary people, through action and compassion, can lead quite extraordinary lives; two people who really did make the world a better place.

Let me challenge you to do the same and wish you all every happiness and success as you cross over that busy road to the next stage of your lives.

Notes

Notes

Notes

Notes

Also by John Catt Educational...

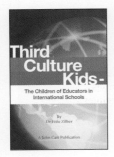

Third Culture Kids – The Children of Educators in International Schools
By Dr Ettie Zilber

The concept of the Third Culture Kids, children who follow their globetrotting parents around the world, is not a new one and has been widely studied. However, there is one specific group of TCKs who have, until now, been largely ignored – EdKids, the children of international school educators.
In this brand new work, Dr Ettie Zilber brings together the material she has collected over many years of research on this unique group and allows them to voice their own opinions, feelings and stories for the first time.

ISBN: 978 1 904724 75 9   Price: £14.99

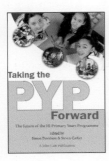

Taking the PYP Forward:
The future of the IB Primary Years Programme
Edited by Simon Davidson & Steven Carber, with an afterword by Dennison J MacKinnon

For the PYP to maintain relevance in education today, inquiry has to be rethought, refreshed and reapplied. *Taking the PYP Forward* does exactly that. Raising many questions and recognising the new challenges facing educators, this collaborative work brings together voices from both within and outside of the PYP.

ISBN 978 1 904724 71 1   Price: £14.95

NEW

Effective Marketing Communication and Development

The *Effective International School* series is a practical service provided by ECIS/CIS, to actively assist schools in their commitment to the promotion of an international outlook amongst all members of their communities.

This newly-published tenth volume offers advice to help bring a common purpose and understanding to the role of marketing, communications and development in an international school setting, and includes guidelines for those just getting started in the field, as well as examples of best practice to inspire even the most seasoned professional.

ISBN: 978 1 904724 81 0   **Price: £14.99**

Pastoral Work and those who practise it: Essays in Leadership in Changing Times

Edited by Hilary Moriarty and Nigel Richardson

The fifth volume in the *Leading Schools* series, following on from previous titles' which focused on the work of Heads; senior management teams; heads of department and newly-qualified teachers.

Written by people in a wide variety of school roles, the book is underpinned by two important issues: first, that pastoral matters have never been more important in schools; and secondly, that the independent school sector can encourage individuality, even in an age when government legislation and the importance of public exam results risk making schools much more uniform in their focus.

ISBN: 978 1 904724 80 3   **Price: £12.50**

Also by George Walker...

Globalization means that no country can afford to ignore what goes on outside its borders. International exchanges are a part of everyday life. As a result, international education has been growing at an astonishing rate over the last generation.

As it continues to develop, few people are better placed to understand the complexities and enormous challenges it faces than Professor George Walker, former director-general of the International Baccalaureate.

"A teacher to teachers, a headmaster to heads of schools, an academic to academics, a parent to parents and yes, to students young and old… George Walker has the rare ability to translate his thoughts, reading and observations into the written word in a way that can be readily understood and enjoyed."

Greg Crafter, 2002 President of the Council of Foundation of the IB

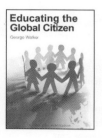

Educating the Global Citizen
In *Educating the Global Citizen*, the third of a series of his lectures to be published by John Catt Educational Ltd, he examines in depth the basic concepts of international education: the apparent tension between human diversity and our common humanity; the importance of intercultural understanding; and the search for a set of universal values to unite humankind.

ISBN: 1 904724 40 X   Price £11.95

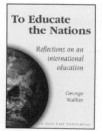

To Educate the Nations
A collection of the lectures and addresses by George Walker, former director-general of the International Baccalaureate, presented throughout the world on the theme of international education.

ISBN: 0 901577 78 2   Price £9.95

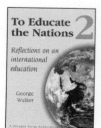

To Educate the Nations 2
The revised and extended edition of *To Educate the Nations*.

ISBN: 1 904724 08 6   Price £14.95